Encyclopedia of the Animal World

BIRDS
The Aerial Hunters

Martyn Bramwell

Facts On File
New York • Oxford

Distributed by
World Book, Inc.

THE AERIAL HUNTERS
The Encyclopedia of the Animal World:
Birds

Managing Editor: Lionel Bender
Art Editor: Ben White
Text Editor: Madeleine Samuel
Project Editor: Graham Bateman
Production: Clive Sparling, Joanna
 Turner

Media conversion and typesetting:
 Robert and Peter MacDonald,
 Una Macnamara

AN EQUINOX BOOK

Planned and produced by:
Equinox (Oxford) Limited,
Musterlin House, Jordan Hill Road,
Oxford OX2 8DP, England

Prepared by Lionheart Books

Library of Congress
Cataloging-in-Publication Data
Bramwell, Martyn.
Birds: the aerial hunters/Martyn Bramwell
p. cm. — — (The Encyclopedia of the
 animal world)
Includes index.
Summary: Provides brief descriptions of
predatory and insectivorous birds.

1. Birds of prey – Juvenile literature.
[1. Birds of prey.]   I. Title. II. Series.

QL696.F3B73 1989   598'.91 - dc19
88-33319 CIP AC

ISBN 0-8160-1963-0

Published in North America by
Facts On File, Inc.,
460 Park Avenue South,
New York, N.Y. 10016

Origination by Alpha Reprographics Ltd,
Perivale, Middx, England

Printed in Hong Kong

10 9 8 7 6 5 4 3 2

FACT PANEL: Key to symbols denoting general features of animals

SYMBOLS WITH NO WORDS

Activity time

● Nocturnal

● Daytime

◐ Dawn/Dusk

○ All the time

Group size

▪ Solitary

▫ Pairs

◨ Small groups (up to 10)

■ Flocks

◤ Variable

Conservation status

☠ All species threatened

☠ Some species threatened

No species threatened (no symbol)

SYMBOLS NEXT TO HEADINGS

Habitat

◧ General

◤ Mountain/Moorland

◢ Desert

〰 Sea

■ Amphibious

▲ Tundra

◢ Forest/Woodland

● Grassland

❂ Freshwater

Diet

■ Other animals

■ Plants

◪ Animals and Plants

Breeding

◉ Seasonal (at fixed times)

◡ Non-seasonal (at any time)

CONTENTS

PREFACE

The National Wildlife Federation

For the wildlife of the world, 1936 was a very big year. That's when the National Wildlife Federation formed to help conserve the millions of species of animals and plants that call Earth their home. In trying to do such an important job, the Federation has grown to be the largest conservation group of its kind.

Today, plants and animals face more dangers than ever before. As the human population grows and takes over more and more land, the wild places of the world disappear. As people produce more and more chemicals and cars and other products to make life better for themselves, the environment often becomes worse for wildlife.

But there is some good news. Many animals are better off today than when the National Wildlife Federation began. Alligators, wild turkeys, deer, wood ducks, and others are thriving – thanks to the hard work of everyone who cares about wildlife.

The Federation's number one job has always been education. We teach kids the wonders of nature through *Your Big Backyard* and *Ranger Rick* magazines and our annual National Wildlife Week celebration. We teach grown-ups the importance of a clean environment through *National Wildlife* and *International Wildlife* magazines. And we help teachers teach about wildlife with our environmental education activity series called *Naturescope*.

The National Wildlife Federation is nearly five million people, all working as one. We all know that by helping wildlife, we are also helping ourselves. Together we have helped pass laws that have cleaned up our air and water, protected endangered species, and left grand old forests standing tall.

You can help too. Every time you plant a bush that becomes a home to a butterfly, every time you help clean a lake or river of trash, every time you walk instead of asking for a ride in a car – you are part of the wildlife team.

You are also doing your part by learning all you can about the wildlife of the world. That's why the National Wildlife Federation is happy to help bring you this Encyclopedia. We hope you enjoy it.

Jay D. Hair, President
National Wildlife Federation

INTRODUCTION

The Encyclopedia of the Animal World surveys the main groups and species of animals alive today. Written by a team of specialists, it includes the most current information and the newest ideas on animal behavior and survival. The Encyclopedia looks at how the shape and form of an animal reflect its life-style – the ways in which a creature's size, color, feeding methods and defenses have all evolved in relationship to a particular diet, climate and habitat. Discussed also are the ways in which human activities often disrupt natural ecosystems and threaten the survival of many species.

In this Encyclopedia the animals are grouped on the basis of their body structure and their evolution from common ancestors. Thus, there are single volumes or groups of volumes on mammals, birds, reptiles and amphibians, fish, insects and so on. Within these major categories, the animals are grouped according to their feeding habits or general life-styles. Because there is so much information on the animals in two of these major categories, there are four volumes devoted to mammals (*The Small Plant-Eaters*; *The Hunters*; *The Large Plant-Eaters*; *Primates, Insect-Eaters and Baleen Whales*) and three to birds (*The Waterbirds*; *The Aerial Hunters*; *The Plant- and Seed-Eaters*).

This volume, *Birds – The Aerial Hunters*, includes entries on eagles, hawks, vultures, owls, swifts, woodpeckers, flycatchers, wagtails, wrens, warblers and tits. (Aquatic hunters, such as penguins, and terrestrial hunters and scavengers, for example crows, are dealt with in other volumes.) Together they number almost 4,000 species. These birds feed almost entirely on other animals. Some of the larger species, such as the eagles and vultures, may seem to be fierce and frightening. But others, for example the wagtails, pipits, wrens, nuthatches and treecreepers, are very gentle, and most species of warblers, thrushes, larks, woodpeckers, tits and chickadees are familiar birds of parks and gardens.

Perhaps best known among the aerial hunters are the so-called birds of prey, or raptors (from the Latin meaning plunderers). These include the osprey, falcons, hawks, buzzards, eagles and vultures. They all share the same specializations for finding food and for holding and tearing apart the bodies of other animals: acute vision, strong legs and feet, mostly equipped with sharp curved claws, and a hooked beak. Most of these birds hunt by day. Other aerial hunters, among them most owls and the swifts, are nocturnal predators – they feed mainly at night or at dusk and dawn.

While the birds of prey eat fish, mammals, reptiles and other large prey – either dead (carrion) or alive – many aerial hunters feed mainly on insects. These include the nightjars, swallows, woodpeckers, lyrebirds, pittas, cuckoos and larks. Among these, cuckoos are notorious as nest parasites – the females lay their eggs in the nests of other birds and leave the nest owners to bring up their young for them.

Each article in this Encyclopedia is devoted to an individual species or group of closely related species. The text starts with a short scene-setting story that highlights one or more of the animal's unique features. It then continues with details of the most interesting aspects of the animal's physical features and abilities, diet and feeding behavior, and general life-style. It also covers conservation and the animal's relationships with people.

A fact panel provides easy reference to the main features of distribution (natural, not introductions to other areas by humans), habitat, diet, size, color and breeding. (An explanation of the color-coded symbols is given on page 2 of the book.) The panel also includes a list of the common and scientific (Latin) names of species mentioned in the main text and photo captions. For species illustrated in major artwork panels but not described elsewhere, the names are given in the caption accompanying the artwork. In such illustrations, all animals are shown to scale; actual dimensions may be found in the text. To help the reader appreciate the size of the animals, in the upper right part of the page at the beginning of an article are scale drawings comparing the size of the species with that of a human being (or of a human foot).

Many species of animal are threatened with extinction as a result of human activities. In this Encyclopedia the following terms are used to show the status of a species as defined by the International Union for the Conservation of Nature and Natural Resources:

Endangered – in danger of extinction unless their habitat is no longer destroyed and they are not hunted by people.

Vulnerable – likely to become endangered in the near future.

Rare – exist in small numbers but neither endangered nor vulnerable at present.

A glossary provides definitions of technical terms used in the book. A common name and scientific (Latin) name index provide easy access to text and illustrations.

EAGLES

High above the Appalachian Mountains of eastern North America, a Golden eagle hangs almost motionless in a clear summer sky. Far below it sees an ideal hunting spot – a long ridge covered with open grassy vegetation. The eagle glides down, and flies fast and low along one side of the ridge. Suddenly it swoops up and over the crest. Fifty yards away, on the other side of the ridge, a hare is feeding, completely unaware of the danger. It has no chance. Even as the hare turns to run, the aerial hunter strikes, killing it outright with its talons.

EAGLES Accipitridae (part of family) *(53 species)*

Size: length 16-48in; weight 1-14½lb.

Plumage: plain gray, brown, or striking combinations of dark brown and white. Forest species often with black and white bars on wings.

Species mentioned in text:
African fish eagle (*Haliaeetus vocifer*)
Bald eagle (*Haliaeetus leucocephalus*)
Bateleur (*Terathopius ecaudatus*)
Booted eagle (*Hieraaetus pennatus*)
Golden eagle (*Aquila chrysaetos*)
Little eagle (*Hieraaetus morphnoides*)
Martial eagle (*Polemaetus bellicosus*)
Vulturine fish eagle or Palm-nut vulture (*Gypohierax angolensis*)
White-bellied sea eagle (*Haliaeetus leucogaster*)

Habitat: all land habitats, also sea coasts, lakes.

Diet: mammals, birds, fish and reptiles; also carrion.

Breeding: most species 1 or 2 eggs, incubated for 32-60 days.

The Golden eagle is one of the largest members of a group of 30 species of birds of prey called the booted eagles. These birds get their name from the fact that their legs are covered with feathers right down to the foot, instead of being bare and scaly like those of all the other eagles. They are also known as "true" eagles.

The booted eagles are a varied group indeed. The smallest is probably the Little eagle of Australasia, which weighs around 1lb. Unlike many of its open-country relatives, this tiny hunter inhabits forests and well-wooded regions. It hunts by dropping on to its prey either from flight about 30ft above the ground, or from a perch in a leafy tree. Because of its small size it concentrates mainly on young rabbits, ground-dwelling birds and occasionally lizards.

MAMMAL-KILLER
At the other end of the scale is the magnificent Martial eagle of Africa, which can have a wingspan of well over 6½ft and weigh up to 14½lb. It lives in the savannah and thornbush country south of the Sahara Desert, and is even found in semi-desert regions. This eagle spends a great deal of its time on the wing, soaring for hours at a time on the currents of hot air that rise over the Sun-baked hills and plains. Often the bird will fly so high that it appears as little more than a speck from the ground.

Because food is widely scattered over the huge African grasslands, a

◀A European Booted eagle with young. This small eagle, weighing about 1¼lb, inhabits wooded mountains and ravines.

▲An adult Golden eagle in Finland. Here, as in 13 other European countries, the bird is protected by law.

▼The female Little eagle incubates her one or two eggs by herself, but her mate usually brings food to her on the nest.

pair of Martial eagles may require a hunting territory of up to 50 sq miles. The birds usually hunt in one area for a few days and then move on to a new location. In some regions Martial eagles prey mainly on large birds such as guineafowl and bustards. In other regions they take mainly mammals, for example hyraxes. However, these powerful birds will also take prey as big as monkeys and goats.

The Martial eagle may occasionally hunt from a perch, but its main method is to spot a target from high in the sky and then attack in a long fast slanting dive that takes the victim completely by surprise.

WRONGLY ACCUSED?

The most widespread and numerous of the world's large eagles is the Golden eagle. It inhabits mountain country right across Europe, Asia and North Africa, and is the only booted eagle found in North America.

In some parts of Europe and North America the Golden eagle has been persecuted by people, mainly because of an undeserved reputation for killing lambs. Lamb carcasses are occasionally found in eagle nests, but although some may be the result of eagle kills, most of the lambs have probably been found already dead. Golden eagles do take some carrion as well as live prey. Their main diet, though, is made up of rabbits and hares, and in North America ground squirrels are often taken. In places where mammals are hard to find, game birds such as grouse and ptarmigan are the main source of food. They are usually caught on the ground, but the Golden eagle can also catch a grouse in flight.

Golden eagle pairs usually have two or three nests on their territory. The nests are called eyries, and are huge constructions made of sticks, placed on rocky ledges high on mountain cliffs. The female usually hatches two chicks, but the first one to hatch often kills the other within the first 2 weeks.

FISH- AND FRUIT-EATERS
Among the most spectacular large eagles are the fishing eagles (11 species) from the Old World and North America. As their name suggests, these birds inhabit coastal regions and the shores of lakes, where they feed on fish, waterbirds and carrion. The only North American species is the Bald eagle – America's national bird. This makes the biggest nest of any eagle. One nest, known to be 36 years old, was 8½ft across and 13ft high.

Unlike the osprey, which plunges into the water to catch its prey, the fishing eagles normally snatch their prey close to the surface in a graceful low-level swoop. The one exception in the group is the Vulturine fish eagle or Palm-nut vulture of Africa. The bird does catch fish, but its main food is the fruit of the oil palm tree, and it is never found far from these trees.

SNAKE- AND SERPENT-KILLERS
The snake eagles are a specialized group of 12 species of hunters found in southern Europe, Africa, central and South-east Asia. They have large, owl-like heads, huge yellow eyes, and short toes for grasping their thin-bodied prey. They hunt mainly from perches and drop swiftly on to snakes, frogs and lizards on the ground.

This group also has its odd-bird-out. The magnificent bateleur has black, white and chestnut plumage and such a short tail that it appears in flight like an enormous flying wing. It hunts by gliding across the African plains at speeds of up to 50mph in search of small mammals, birds, carrion and snakes.

▶ Until recently the southern race of the American Bald eagle was an endangered species. Now its future appears safe, due to strict conservation laws.

▲►Talons outstretched, a White-bellied sea eagle closes in on its target (top). Moments after the strike (center) its legs are dragged backwards by the weight of the fish, but even a one-footed grip (bottom) is enough to secure the catch.

◄In their spectacular courtship display a pair of African fish eagles grasp each other's talons as they tumble downward through the air like falling leaves.

HAWKS AND BUZZARDS

HAWKS AND BUZZARDS Accipitridae
(part of family) (*150 species*)

● ☠

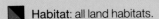 Habitat: all land habitats.

■ Diet: mammals, birds, snakes, frogs, insects.

○ Breeding: small species lay 5-7 eggs, large species 1 or 2; incubation period 32 and 120 days respectively.

Size: most species: length 12-28in, weight 1-9lb; largest (Harpy eagle): length 40in, weight 13lb.

Plumage: very variable, but most species gray or brown, darker above than below.

Species mentioned in text:
Augur buzzard (*Buteo rufofuscus*)
Bat hawk (*Machieramphus alcinus*)
Black kite (*Milvus migrans*)
Common buzzard (*Buteo buteo*)
Cooper's hawk (*Accipiter cooperii*)
Crane hawk (*Geranospiza caerulescens*)
Harpy eagle (*Harpia harpyia*)
Hen, or Northern, harrier (*Circus cyaneus*)
Northern goshawk (*Accipiter gentilis*)
Philippine eagle (*Pithecophaga jefferyi*)
Red-shouldered hawk (*Buteo lineatus*)
Red-tailed hawk (*B. jamaicensis*)
Sharp-shinned hawk (*Accipiter striatus*)
Snail kite (*Rostrhamus sociabilis*)

As darkness falls over a small island in South-east Asia, millions of bats stream out of caves hidden in the depths of the rain forest. Most of them will spend the night feeding, but for some there is danger. Lying in ambush is a Bat hawk, one of Asia's most specialized hawks. Picking its target the hunter dashes in. One strike is enough. The hawk swerves away, transferring its catch from its claws to its bill as it heads back to its nest.

The Bat hawk is found in the rain forests of Malaysia, Sumatra, Borneo and New Guinea, and also in tropical Africa. It is the only known specialist bat-hunter among the birds of prey, and it is also unusual in carrying its catch in its bill. That is something much more typical of owls than of hawks.

UNUSUAL DIETS
The Bat hawk belongs to the group of 31 species of bird called the kites and honey buzzards. Among them are a great many unusual and specialized birds. The Snail kite, for example, lives in the swamp forests and marshlands of the Florida Everglades, and its main food consists of the large freshwater snails that abound in that habitat. The bird's bill is finely hooked and pointed – the perfect tool for extracting the snails from their shells.

Like all specialists, though, the Snail kite is much at risk. Vast areas of the Florida wetlands have been drained for housing and other types of development. As the swamps are destroyed the snails too disappear, and along with them go the birds that depend on them for food.

The honey buzzards of Europe, Africa and Asia have found another rich source of food – the ground nests and tree nests of various kinds of bee and wasp. The birds tear open the insects' nests with their claws and feed on the honey and larvae inside. However, the adult insects pack a powerful sting and have to be "disarmed" before they can be eaten. The birds do this by snipping off the back end of each insect's body before it is swallowed. Honey buzzards also prey on worms, frogs, small mammals and birds, and some species eat berries.

A TOWN DWELLER

The Black kite of Europe, Africa and Asia is a complete contrast to its specialized relatives. It is a true all-rounder, preying on insects, fish and worms, but often making its living mainly as a scavenger. In the warmer parts of its range, especially across southern Asia, thousands of Black kites inhabit towns and cities. They are often seen on rubbish heaps and in streets. The birds perch on roofs, telegraph poles and dockside cranes then swoop down to pounce on rats and mice or to snatch food from market stalls. There are even cases of them snatching food from astonished shoppers' hands!

THE CUNNING HARRIERS

It is tempting to imagine that all birds of prey catch their food by means of a fast diving attack or a chase. But that is not so. The 10 species of harrier, for example, are birds of open grasslands

▼ **Medium-sized birds of prey** A Gray chanting goshawk (*Melierax poliopterus*) **(1)** calls from the top of a termite mound. A Black-mantled sparrowhawk (*Accipiter melanochlamys*) **(2)** and Red kite (*Milvus milvus*) **(3)** with prey. A Pied harrier (*Circus melanoleucus*) **(4)** hunting.

and marshes which specialize in slow, low-level flight as their main hunting technique.

Harriers are medium-sized hawks with slim bodies and with long wings and tails that provide the lift and control necessary for low-speed flight. They often fly at speeds as low as 18mph, and if a harrier is flying into a light head-wind it may be moving over the ground at only 10mph. (A falcon can fly at over 100mph.) With brief periods of hovering, this gives the bird plenty of time to search the ground below for prey. The harriers have rather owl-like faces, and like the owls they rely on accurate hearing to pin-point their prey. They can locate their quarry even when it is hidden from sight among dense vegetation.

The Hen harrier, known as the Northern harrier in North America, is a typical member of the group. It inhabits marshlands and heathlands, and sometimes cornfields too. From the air it silently patrols an area with its wings raised to form an instantly recognizable shallow V-shape. Its diet consists of frogs, mice, large insects, snakes and small birds.

Unlike most other birds of prey the harriers nest on the ground, building

▲ In a North American forest, a young Northern goshawk picks at a Gray squirrel carcass with its hooked beak.

3

4

large mounds of reeds and rushes, well hidden from view. The female does most of the building, but the male helps by collecting nest material. He delivers the material in a most unusual way. Instead of landing at the nest site, he swoops low overhead and drops the material close by, for the female to retrieve. Later, when the eggs have hatched, the male uses the same method to deliver food to the nest for the female and young.

DOUBLE-JOINTED
The two species of harrier-hawk of Africa and the Crane hawk of Central and South America form a group of medium-sized woodland hawks with a unique adapatation for catching their prey. Their legs can bend either way at the middle (tarsal) joint, and this enables the birds to reach into the most awkward crevices in rocks or tree bark to pull out the lizards, frogs, birds' eggs and nestlings that are their main prey. These hawks get into the most unusual positions when searching for food, and will often hang upside down to reach inside a particularly inaccessible tree-hole. At other times they hunt by flying back and forth, scanning the ground below for food, much as the true harriers do.

A FAMILY OF HUNTERS
The family Accipitridae is by far the biggest of the five bird of prey families, and it includes a huge variety of different birds among its 217 species. The eagles (see pages 6-9) and the kites, harrier-hawks and harriers we have met so far are all fairly small groups. Together they make up just over half of the total number of species. The two biggest groups are the sparrowhawks and goshawks, and the buzzards and harpies, each of which contains 53 species.

WOODLAND PREDATORS
The sparrowhawks and goshawks are small- to medium-sized birds found in

▲A sparrowhawk broods her young in the rain. Like many northern birds of prey, the sparrowhawk is very slowly recovering from the damage to wildlife inflicted by pesticides.

forest, woodland and scrub habitats all over the world. Their wings are short and rounded and their tails are long. These adaptations enable the birds to dash through dense woody vegetation at a breakneck pace, using agility, speed and surprise to run down their prey.

Cooper's hawk is typical of the whole group. It inhabits woodlands of North America from Canada south to Mexico, often roosting perched on one leg in a coniferous tree, but nearly always choosing deciduous woods at nesting time. Its hunting methods are a mixture of skill, speed and trickery. Often the hawk will fly to a partly concealed perch and wait there until a bird or squirrel wanders out into the open, unaware of danger. Then it

dashes out, using its long legs to reach out and snatch the victim on the ground or as it tries to flee.

SWOOPING AND POUNCING
As in most species of sparrowhawk, the female Cooper's hawk is much larger than the male, and while male birds prey on starlings, blackbirds and flickers, the females will take prey as big as grouse.

Both males and females are skilled at using natural cover to get close to their prey. Even a group of birds feeding on the ground in a clearing can be taken by surprise. The hawk swoops in low, using every tree stump, bush and dip in the ground to conceal its approach.

Birds are sometimes deliberately flushed out of cover. The hawk will fly straight towards a bush, then dodge sideways at the last minute, dashing round to the far side to pounce on any birds frightened into coming into the open.

RETURN JOURNEYS

As the abundance of food begins to decline in the fall, the most northerly Cooper's hawks migrate southwards. Some travel as far as Colombia. As they head south they often join with other hawks – Sharp-shinned, Red-tailed and other unrelated species. The southward mass migration of birds of prey down the "flyway" of the Appalachian Mountains is one of the greatest birdwatching sights in the USA.

The birds return in February and March, usually to the same patch of woodland, although a new nest is made each year. Males and females perform courtship display flights, and the nest-building and mating is accompanied by much displaying and the singing of duets.

BUZZARDS AND HAWKS

The buzzards and their relatives are a very varied group, both in size and in habitat. They range from tiny woodland hawks to the world's biggest, most powerful, and probably rarest birds of prey.

The Common buzzard breeds in woodland, but often hunts over open moorland, plains and mountains. It is found right across Europe and Asia, as far east as Siberia and Japan, but like many birds of prey the buzzard is a migrant. Each year the northern populations move from their summer breeding areas to winter quarters in Africa, India and South-east Asia.

The buzzard is much less striking in color than its hawk relatives, and spends a lot of time either perched on a fence-post or tree, or slowly soaring back and forth along a rocky hillside as it searches for rodents and small rabbits.

►Proudly perched on a rocky ledge, a Common buzzard, the most common European bird of prey, surveys its habitat.

In North America, the buzzard's relatives include the handsome Red-shouldered hawk and the Red-tailed hawk. The Red-shouldered hawk inhabits damp lowland forests and marshland in the eastern half of the country. It feeds mainly on mice, frogs and small snakes. The Red-tailed hawk prefers upland regions. Its diet consists primarily of small mammals.

Like several other American species of hawk, these birds have suffered in recent years from the harmful effects of pesticides widely used on agricultural land.

◄The spiky head plume of the Philippine monkey-eating eagle gives the bird an oddly human face.

KINGS OF THE FOREST

Pride of place in the entire bird of prey family must go to the Harpy eagle. This formidable aerial hunter inhabits the lowland tropical forests of South America from southern Mexico to northern Argentina. Despite its great size it is an agile hunter. When hunting it threads its way through the canopy of the Amazon jungle at up to 40mph, pursuing the monkeys that make up a large part of its diet. The Harpy eagle also preys on sloths, opossums and tree porcupines. It will also take snakes and large birds when the opportunity comes along.

Details of the Harpy eagle's breeding behavior are not well known, but the Harpy's nest is a huge structure of sticks, lined with green leaves. This is

▲Tail fanned like the flaps of an airplane, an Augur buzzard swoops low. This aerial hunter is the most common buzzard of East and southern Africa.

placed in a tree fork usually 130 to 150ft above the ground.

In the rain forests of the Philippines lives another magnificent predator, the Philippine "monkey-eating" eagle. In every way it is the Asian counterpart of its South American relative – huge, magnificent and, sadly, now listed as an endangered species. Nobody knows how many Harpies survive in Amazonia. In the Philippines there are probably no more than 200 monkey-eating eagles left. In the past, hunting for zoo specimens and trophies was the main threat. Today it is the destruction of the birds' native forests.

FALCONS

A Peregrine falcon shows off its speed and agility in flight as it homes in on a wood-pigeon. Its hunting dive or "stoop" is a breath-taking power dive that reaches speeds of over 125 mph.

▲ **Three of the world's falcons** The Barred forest falcon (*Micrastur ruficollis*) (1) of tropical South America, an Aplomado falcon (*Falco femoralis*) (2) of Mexico and South America, and the Eurasian kestrel (3).

FALCONS Falconidae (*60 species*)

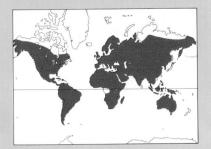

● ▣ ꙮ

◧ **Habitat:** very varied, from sea coasts to grassland, woodland, tropical forest and deserts.

▣ **Diet:** mammals, birds, reptiles, insects; also carrion.

◎ **Breeding:** caracaras 2 or 3 eggs, laid in a nest. True falcons up to 9 eggs, (usually 4 or 5), laid on bare rock, in a rough scrape, or in an abandoned nest. Incubation period up to 30 days.

Size: smallest (Asian falconets): length 6in, weight 1½ ounces; largest (caracaras): length 14-24in, weight ¾-3½lb.

Plumage: varied; usually brown or gray, and dark above, pale below. Many species with strong colors and bold markings.

Species mentioned in text:
American kestrel (*Falco sparverius*)
Eurasian kestrel (*F. tinnunculus*)
Gyrfalcon (*F. rusticolus*)
Lanner falcon (*F. biarmicus*)
Mauritius kestrel (*F. punctatus*)
Peregrine falcon (*F. peregrinus*)
Red-throated caracara (*Daptrius americanus*)

The Peregrine falcon is the most widespread and successful of all the birds of prey. It is found in every continent except Antarctica, and on many of the world's island groups too. It is one of the biggest members of the falcon family, measuring up to 20in long. With its gray-blue back, beautifully banded pale buff undersides, yellow eye-rings and black "mustache," it is also one of the most handsome.

SPEED AND PRECISION
The superb hunting skills of the Peregrine falcon have made it the favorite bird of falconers in many countries. The birds are caught in flight using nets and then trained. They can be used to hunt gamebirds the size of bustards. The Peregrine's hunting method is unique. Unlike the hawks, which usually attack in fast level flight and strike with their front toes, the Peregrine plummets down on to its prey in a dive that has been estimated at speeds ranging from 100mph to a staggering 250mph.

Just before reaching its target the Peregrine slows and levels out, striking the lethal blow with the needle-sharp talons of its rear "toes." The victim is often allowed to tumble to the ground, but the attacker closely follows it. The Peregrine's main prey varies according to where it lives, but its favorite quarry includes pigeons, grouse and small sea-birds. Young Peregrines take smaller prey such as finches.

The Peregrine falcon is found in many different habitats. It seems to prefer rocky crags, and is most common on rocky sea coasts. But it is a versatile bird, and is also found in moorland, open grassland, scrub and desert areas, and even in forests.

A YEAR IN THE LIFE
There are 18 separate races of Peregrine falcon, living in regions as varied as Alaskan river valleys and the

tropical grasslands of Africa. The tropical species are year-round residents, but most northern birds migrate in winter to areas with better food supplies. European birds migrate to southern Africa, and North American birds fly far into South America.

▼A Eurasian kestrel returns to its young with a large rodent. Like most falcons it does not build a proper nest.

At the start of the breeding season the male Peregrine chooses a good breeding ledge on a cliff. When he sees a female he flies out, calling to her, then returns to the ledge. The performance is repeated until a female accepts the male's invitation. After that the two birds swoop and dive and chase each other in a spectacular series of display flights. The birds make no nest and the eggs are

simply laid on the bare rock. The male usually shares the task of incubating the eggs, and also brings food to the nest for himself and the female.

THE PESTICIDE THREAT

During the 1960s the Peregrine populations of North America and Europe began to fall alarmingly. Scientists then discovered that the shells of the birds' eggs were so thin and fragile

▼ ◄A Peregrine falcon with young at a typical mountain nest-site. The Peregrine was one of 20 species of falcon badly affected by DDT in the 1960s. The photograph on the left shows the weakening effect the chemical had on the shells of the bird's eggs.

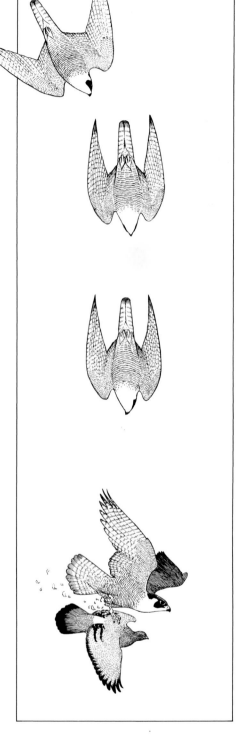

that they were breaking when the incubating birds sat on them. The cause was DDT, a common farm pesticide. The chemical was building up in the bodies of seed- and insect-eating birds, and it passed on to the falcons when they ate these birds.

Many countries have now banned the use of DDT, and in these the Peregrine is making a recovery. (In the developing countries of the tropics and subtropics especially, the use of DDT is on the increase.) It was a sharp lesson in the dangers of using chemicals that remain in the environment long after their job has been done.

THE SMALLER FALCONS

The Peregrine, and the magnificent gray and white gyrfalcon of the Arctic wastelands, are two of the bigger falcons. But there are many smaller species too. One of the most familiar in Europe is the kestrel. This is often seen hovering over the verges of motorways.

The kestrel holds its position in the air with rapid beats of its long pointed wings and with constant adjustments to the angle of its unusually long fan-shaped tail. It is the only falcon to hunt in this way, scanning the ground below for the mice, frogs and small

▲Folding back its wings to reduce air resistance, a Peregrine falcon plunges in a near-vertical dive. If it misses its quarry, or is simply "playing," it swoops up again and repeats the attack.

breeds well in captivity, and several captive-bred birds have already been reintroduced to the few remaining patches of forest. The species may just survive, but only with total protection for the bird and its habitat – and a good deal of luck.

Smaller still are the pygmy falcons and falconets. One species inhabits the desert areas and grasslands of northern Argentina. There are two pygmy species, one inhabiting woodlands in southern Asia, the other living in the desert and thornbush country of Africa. But smallest of all – barely 6in from bill to the tail tip – are the falconets of tropical Asia. These sparrow-sized hunters are boldly colored, with black above and white or chestnut-brown below. Their main prey are the large forest dragonflies and moths, usually caught on the wing in a darting attack from a perch.

SOUTH AMERICAN COUSINS

The caracaras are large (buzzard-sized) birds with long legs and broad wings. At first glance it is hard to think of them as falcons. Unlike their dashing relatives they are rather slow, sluggish birds that spend much of their time either perched in the trees or walking about on the ground.

The caracaras are found only in South America, where they inhabit open country, woodland, forest and grassland. They feed mainly on large insects, but they are also carrion-eaters and are often seen in the company of New World vultures, squabbling over the remains of an animal carcass.

The Red-throated caracara is rather vulture-like in appearance. Its plumage is glossy black, shot with green and blue. Its cheeks and throat are bright red and bare of feathers, and it has a habit of perching on a branch screaming and cackling loudly. Its feeding habits are just as strange as it specializes in tearing open wasps' nests to feed on the larvae.

▲ The Lanner falcon of Africa and the Mediterranean often attacks its prey head-on, instead of approaching from above or behind as most falcons do.

birds like larks, pipits and buntings that make up its diet.

The Eurasian kestrel is mainly a bird of grasslands, heaths and open farmland. The American kestrel inhabits much drier country and is even found in the desolate desert around Lima in Peru. There the bird preys on lizards, scorpions and large insects. In the gentler climate of North America it feeds mainly on grasshoppers and other large insects in summer and on

mice and small birds like sparrows during the winter months.

LIZARD- AND MOTH-EATERS

The Mauritius kestrel is now one of the rarest birds in the world. It is a forest-dwelling species, with short rounded wings that are perfectly adapted for twisting and turning among tree trunks and branches. The bird hunts for tree-lizards, beetles and flying insects. Sadly, most of the forest has been cut down for its valuable timber, and for farmland. In 1985 there were only 16 breeding pairs left in the wild. Fortunately this kestrel

OSPREY

Cruising about 130ft above the waters of an Alaskan lake, a hunting osprey scans the area below for signs of fish. Suddenly it spots a big salmon swimming near the surface. The osprey hovers for a moment, then plunges in a steep dive. It hits the water feet first in a cloud of spray. Moments later it reappears, shaking the water from its feathers before climbing away with the fish in its talons.

This spectacular hunting dive is the osprey's speciality. The bird's legs and feet are exceptionally strong to take the force of the crash dives, and its feet are specially adapted to grasp its slippery prey. The four toes on each foot end in hooked talons, and their undersides are covered with horny spines to improve their grip.

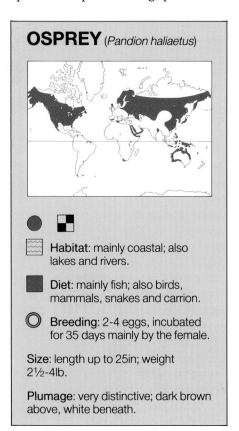

OSPREY (*Pandion haliaetus*)

● ◼

〰️ **Habitat:** mainly coastal; also lakes and rivers.

◼ **Diet:** mainly fish; also birds, mammals, snakes and carrion.

◯ **Breeding:** 2-4 eggs, incubated for 35 days mainly by the female.

Size: length up to 25in; weight 2½-4lb.

Plumage: very distinctive; dark brown above, white beneath.

A fish caught by an osprey rarely gets away. The bird's grip is so good that it sometimes cannot let go of its quarry even when it wants to. There are reports of ospreys being dragged underwater when they have taken on fish that were just too big for them!

Adult ospreys usually take prey weighing up to 1lb, but occasionally they will catch fish up to 3½lb – almost as heavy as themselves.

THE WORLDWIDE HUNTER

The osprey is the most widespread of the large birds of prey. It breeds in North America, Europe, Africa, Asia and Australia, and also on many small islands. South America is the only continent where the osprey does not breed, but even there it is a common winter visitor on migration from North America. Individuals from northern Europe and Asia migrate to Africa for the winter.

In some regions the osprey lives near lakes and rivers, but in others it inhabits coastal lagoons, marshes and mangroves. It feeds mainly on fish, but will also catch small mammals, birds, sea snakes and even sea snails.

MATING FOR LIFE

Ospreys are not ready to breed until they are 3 to 4 years old, but once they have found a mate they remain together for life. To attract a mate, the male bird performs a stunning display flight. He climbs high into the sky with a fish in his talons, calling loudly. He hovers for a moment, then folds his wings and plummets earthwards. The display is often repeated many times before the bird rests.

Once the male and female have paired, they build a huge nest of sticks. The nest is usually perched on top of a tall tree or a high rock outcrop with a

▶A male osprey returns to its nest on a mangrove tree in the Red Sea. The birds nearly always carry their prey head forwards to reduce wind resistance.

▲ Just before it hits the water, the osprey swings its feet forwards to strike the target with outstretched talons.

good view over the fishing grounds. The same nest is repaired and re-used year after year.

The eggs are incubated mainly by the female, and hatch after about 35 days. The next 5 to 6 weeks are hard work for the male. His job is to bring a constant supply of fish to the nest. There, the female tears them up and feeds them to the chicks. Once the youngsters are big enough to feed themselves, both parents share the work of hunting.

A CONSERVATION SUCCESS

Although the osprey is common in some parts of the world, in others it has suffered from hunting, and from the poisoning of its food by farm chemicals such as DDT. These deadly chemicals are washed into rivers and seas from the land.

In Britain, the native ospreys were completely wiped out by 1908, but after a gap of almost 50 years the birds were seen again in the Scottish Highlands. In 1955, one pair attempted to nest. They were not successful that year, but the nest site was protected by conservation organizations, and in 1959 the first young ospreys were born. Since then the population has grown to about 40 pairs.

VULTURES

In 1987, in the foothills of the Sierra Nevada, California, a group of scientists watched a huge black-and-white vulture circling slowly in the sky. It was a sad day. Their job was to catch the last California condor in the wild. Years of shooting, trapping and poisoning had almost wiped out this magnificent species, and the only hope for its survival was to take the remaining birds into the safety of California's zoos.

All the 27 surviving California condors are now in captivity. Their close relative the Andean condor is more fortunate. It is still widespread in the mountains of western South America.

These two species, and five others, make up the group called the New World vultures. The group ranges from southern Canada to the tip of South America. They are not closely

VULTURES Cathartidae
(7 species), Accipitridae *(14 species)*

⬤   ◨   ⚐

⬛ **Habitat:** grassland, desert, mountain and other open areas; some species in forest.

⬛ **Diet:** mainly carrion; small mammals, birds' eggs and fruit. Some species frequent rubbish heaps.

◯ **Breeding:** condors: 1 egg every 2 years; most species 1-3 eggs, laid on ground or rock ledge;

incubated for up to 50 days and nestling period up to 120 days depending on species. Only Old World vultures build nests.

Size: length 24-56in; weight 2-30lb. Wingspan up to 10ft.

Plumage: mainly dark brown to black, often with paler patches on the underside of the wings; some species partly white.

Species mentioned in text:
Andean condor (*Vultur gryphus*)
Bearded vulture or lammergeier (*Gypaetus barbatus*)
California condor (*Vultur californianus*)
Egyptian vulture (*Neophron percnopterus*)
European black vulture (*Aegypius monarchus*)
Griffon vulture (*Gyps fulvus*)
King vulture (*Sarcoramphus papa*)
Rüppell's griffon (*Gyps rueppelli*)
Secretary bird (*Sagittarius serpentarius*)

▲ The Bearded vulture feeds on the marrow of animal bones, which it breaks open by dropping them on to rocks from a great height. This species is sometimes called the lammergeier.

▲ The King vulture inhabits dense tropical rain forests in Central and South America. It finds food in the forest by following other scavenging animals to it.

▼ A Secretary bird finishing off a snake. The bird probably got its name from its head plumes, which look like quill pens tucked behind the ear of an old-fashioned secretary or clerk.

related to the vultures of Africa and Asia, but they look similar, with bald heads and necks, massive bills, and long broad wings. They also have a similar life-style, soaring high on currents of air, scanning the ground with sharp eyes as they search for carrion (dead animals), which is their main food.

The condors nest on cliff ledges and in caves high in the mountains. Their smaller relatives nest on the ground among the grassland and scrub vegetation of the foothills.

THE OLD WORLD VULTURES

The vultures of Asia and Africa are also mainly scavengers, feeding on the carcasses of animals that have died or been killed by predators. They are usually most active during the hottest part of the day, when they can "ride" the warm air currents (thermals) that rise over desert lands, or the swirling winds in mountain regions. When a vulture spots a carcass, it begins to

◄ Rüppell's griffons in Kenyan grassland feeding on a wildebeest carcass. In half an hour nothing will remain but bones. The birds normally eat only very fresh meat.

circle lower. Its neighbors notice this, and fly towards the scene. Within minutes, vultures are converging from all directions.

These vultures vary in their social behavior. A few, like the Griffon vulture of Europe and Asia, often breed in colonies of several hundred pairs, with nests only a few yards apart. The birds may fly 100 miles from a colony in search of food. Others, like the European black vulture, live in pairs, nesting in trees or on cliffs in widely separated territories. They feed much closer to home, and often take live prey as well as carrion.

The Egyptian vulture is a relatively small bird with mainly white plumage, found in desert and farmland in North Africa and the Middle East. It is not big enough to compete with larger vultures over carcasses so instead it uses speed and agility to dash in and snatch a morsel when it can. It

is also known to smash open ostrich eggs by throwing stones at them.

SNAKE-KILLER

The Secretary bird is so unusual that scientists have placed it in a family all of its own. With its long legs and long tail it looks rather like a heron or stork when it is flying. But it is a true bird of prey, with a very unusual life-style.

Secretary birds are found only on the grasslands of Africa, where they stride through the long grass in search of their favorite prey – snakes. They also eat locusts and grasshoppers, small mammals and birds' eggs, but snake-killing is their speciality. The reptile is often killed by a single kick to the head, but sometimes a long fight takes place, with the Secretary bird battering the snake with its wings as it tries to bite. A stunned snake may be carried into the air and dropped on to the ground to finally kill it.

OWLS

Hunting across open farmland on a moonlit night, the Barn owl looks like a ghostly giant moth. Its softly feathered wings make no sound as it scans the ground listening for the slightest rustling of a mouse in the grass. When the owl makes its attack, it is a silent swooping glide. At the last moment the owl swings its talons forwards to kill its prey.

OWLS Tytonidae (*10 species*), Strigidae (*123 species*)

○ ▣ 🦉

◣ **Habitat:** woodland, forest, grassland, desert, farmland.

◼ **Diet:** small rodents, birds, lizards, insects, frogs, fish.

◎ **Breeding:** 1-14 eggs depending on food supply (usually 2-6). Eggs hatch after 15-35 days according to species. Nestling period up to 56 days.

Size: typical owls: length 5-28in, weight 1½ ounces-9lb; barn owls: length 9-21in, weight ½-3lb. Females usually bigger than males.

Plumage: mainly mottled brown or gray. One species white; several black and white.

Species mentioned in text:
Barn owl (*Tyto alba*)
Burrowing owl (*Athene cunicularia*)
Eagle owl (*Bubo bubo*)
Elf owl (*Micrathene whitneyi*)
Little owl (*Athene noctua*)

The Barn owl is the most widespread of the world's owls. It is found on every continent except Antarctica, and many small islands have their own local race of the bird, found there and nowhere else.

In many ways the Barn owl is representative of all owls. It has a short rounded body and a large head, with big forward-pointing eyes located on the front of its face. Its body and wings are covered with soft feathers that make barely a sound as the bird flies.

The bird usually sets out to hunt as night falls, and it flies low along hedgerows, through woodland and over fields. Occasionally it perches for a while, listening intently for the tiny high-pitched noises of mice, voles, shrews and other small mammals scurrying about in the undergrowth. Its ears are its main sensors. The ear openings are hidden beneath the soft plumage on the sides of the owl's head, and they are unusually large for a bird. At the slightest sound, the owl swivels its head from side to side, "homing in" on the source of the noise. When the sound is equally loud in both ears, the owl knows that it is facing directly towards the source. In this way the bird can target its prey with pin-point accuracy.

Unlike most other birds of prey, the owl carries off its prey in its beak, rarely in its claws. Large prey are torn into pieces to eat, but small animals are swallowed whole, head first. The sorting of edible flesh from the hair, teeth, feathers and bones occurs within the owl's stomach. Some time after feeding, the owl coughs up a dry rounded pellet containing all the undigested bits of prey. These pellets are often found littering the ground beneath an owl's favorite feeding perch or nest site.

FAMILY LIFE

Barn owls breed in the spring, and the number of young they raise in a year depends mainly on food supply. The 2 to 6 eggs are always laid one at a time, spread over several days. They hatch

▶The heart-shaped face, black eyes and unusually long bill are characteristic of the Barn owl. Most typical owls have yellow or orange eyes.

▼Burrowing owls live on the grassland plains of America. They take over or even share prairie dog burrows.

in the same order, and the first chicks to be born have a big advantage because the oldest and strongest chicks always get the biggest share of the food. If food is scarce, only the first few chicks may survive. If food is plentiful, all will survive and the parents may even produce a second family later in the year. Breeding owls do not build a proper nest. The females simply lay their eggs on a bed of dirt and old feathers in a hollow tree, a small cave in a rock cliff, or the corner of a barn roof.

PYGMIES AND GIANTS

The Barn owl and its relatives form a rather small family. Most of the world's 133 owl species belong to a much larger family known as the typical owls. They too are spread all over the world, and they include the biggest, the smallest and the most specialized owls.

Smallest of all are the 12 pygmy owls of Europe, Asia, Africa and the Americas. They include the Elf owl of North

America, which stands only 6in tall. It lives in abandoned woodpecker holes in the giant "organ pipe" cacti of the south-western United States and Mexico. It feeds mainly on insects, caught in the air and on the ground, but will also take desert scorpions and spiders.

Not very much bigger, at 9in tall, is the well-named Little owl. This lives in wooded country, farmland, grassland and semi-desert areas all across Europe from Spain to Russia and in parts of North Africa. It hunts mainly at dusk, but is also often seen in daytime, perched on a fence-post or tree, or flying along with its distinctive bobbing flight. It will take mice and small birds, but nearly half its food consists of insects – especially beetles – which it often catches in a curious bounding run across open ground.

At the other end of the scale are giants like the Eagle owl – a powerful night-time hunter standing 28in tall. This preys on mammals as large as Roe deer fawns and on birds as big as buzzards. Like most big predators the Eagle owl requires a large territory during the breeding season, and so neighboring pairs of birds usually nest at least 2½ miles apart. The male and female birds of breeding pairs usually hunt separately. While away from the nest, however, they keep in touch with loud hooting calls that can be heard up to 2 miles away.

ISLAND RARITIES

Because most owls prey on rats, mice, large insects and other pests, they are popular with people everywhere. They are seldom persecuted, yet the world check-list of endangered birds, published in 1988, lists 21 species of owl as being threatened with extinction. Many of these are island dwellers, and nearly all live in tropical forest of some kind. As the forests are cut down for their valuable timber and to make farmland, the native birds are left with nowhere to go.

▶ **Typical owls and barn owls** The Elf owl **(1)** in typical roosting position. A Barking owl (*Ninox connivens*) **(2)** from Australia, with nestlings in a tree hole. A White-faced scops owl (*Otus leucotis*) **(3)** listening for prey. Boreal owl (*Aegolius funereus*) **(4)** catching a vole. The Common bay owl (*Phodilus badius*) **(5)** of South-east Asia. The Spectacled owl (*Pulsatrix perspicillata*) **(6)** of Central and South America. The Malaysian eagle owl (*Bubo sumatranus*) **(7)**. A Spotted wood owl (*Strix seloputo*) **(8)** of South-east Asia being mobbed by smaller birds. Pel's fishing owl (*Scotopelia peli*) **(9)** from Africa – one of the seven large fish-catching specialists found in Africa and Asia.

2

3

4

8

9

27

CUCKOOS

In a Willow warbler's nest in a clump of long grass, a nasty trick is being played. One of the six eggs has hatched, and a blind, featherless chick is thrashing about among the other eggs. The chick gets its back against one of the eggs and begins to push. Up the side of the nest the chick climbs, until eventually the egg topples out and drops to the ground. A young cuckoo is making sure it has no rivals for the food its foster parents will provide.

There are 127 species of cuckoo in the world today. About 45 of them are "nest parasites" – that is, the females lay their eggs in the nests of other birds and leave the nest owners to bring up their young for them.

Many species, like the Common cuckoo described above, have a very ruthless behavior. Their eggs hatch especially quickly for the size of bird, and the cuckoo chick immediately and instinctively throws out any other eggs or chicks that are in the nest.

Other species do not seem so ruth-less. Their chicks do not kill off the competition straight away. They grow very quickly, and because they are so much bigger and stronger than the resident chicks they take most of the food the foster parents bring to the nest. The smaller chicks are often trampled to death, or simply die from lack of food.

A BIG MOUTH TO FEED

The unfortunate bird whose nest is used or "hijacked" in this way is called the host. The reason why the trick

▲An adult Willow warbler feeds a beak-ful of insects to a fledgling cuckoo. Cuckoos often eat the poisonous hairy caterpillars that young warblers favor.

works so well is that each female cuckoo specializes on just one host species; her eggs are an almost perfect copy of the host bird's own eggs.

Curiously, the cuckoos make no attempt to choose hosts of their own size. The Common cuckoo frequently lays its eggs in the nests of Reed warblers, dunnocks and Meadow pip-its – all quite tiny birds compared with the cuckoo. Sometimes the young cuckoo grows so enormous that the tiny foster parent has to perch on the giant baby's head in order to feed it! Fortunately, nature has built in a safeguard to prevent the parent being injured by its powerful young lodger. Most young birds grasp the parent's bill in their own as food is passed over. The young cuckoo keeps its bill wide open until the foster parent has dropped in a caterpillar or other juicy morsel, and does not close it until the adult bird is safely out of harm's way.

A VARIETY OF HABITS

Even the 80 or so species of non-parasitic cuckoo are unusual birds. The anis of tropical South America, for

---

CUCKOOS Cuculidae
(127 species)

Habitat: desert to humid forest; mainly scrub and woodland.

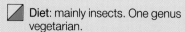 **Diet:** mainly insects. One genus vegetarian.

Breeding: parasitic species lay 10-15 eggs each season, non-parasitic lay 2-5 eggs. Incubation 11-16 days, nestling period 16-24 days.

Size: length 7-26in; weight 1-24 ounces.

Plumage: mainly soft grays and brown. Some species with bars or streaks on underside, or on tail feathers.

Species mentioned in text:
Anis (*Crotophaga* species)
Common cuckoo (*Cuculus canorus*)
Pheasant coucal (*Centropus phasianinus*)
Roadrunner (*Geococcyx californianus*)

▲A selection of cuckoos A Groove-billed ani (*Crotophaga sulcirostris*) **(1)**. Common cuckoo **(2)** removing a host's egg from the nest to make room for its own. A koel (*Eudynamys scolopacea*) from South-east Asia **(3)**. Its chicks share the nest with offspring of the host species. A Yellow-billed cuckoo (*Coccyzus americanus*) from the USA **(4)** sitting on its nest. The Pheasant coucal **(5)**.

example, build a large, ball-shaped nest of sticks in a tree. Each nest contains several quite separate nest chambers, and each one is the private home of a breeding pair of anis.

Another group, the coucals of Africa, Asia and Australia, are large, skulking, ground-dwelling birds. One of these, the Pheasant coucal, usually raises either one or two ugly black nestlings. As in many other cuckoo species, the nestling raises its tail and squirts out a jet of foul-smelling liquid at the first sign of approaching danger. Several other species of coucal build elaborate domed nests and similarly care for their young.

TEMPERATURE REGULATOR
Most unusual of all is the roadrunner, made famous in countless cartoon films. It lives in the desert scrubland of south-western North America, and feeds mainly on large insects and lizards, caught in a darting, high-stepping chase over the dry ground. This species was once heavily perse-cuted in the belief that it was harmful to populations of game birds.

Night-time in the desert can be bitterly cold, and the roadrunner's body is specially adapted to cope with these harsh conditions. Instead of burning up energy keeping its body at normal daytime temperature all through the night, it simply allows its body temperature to fall slightly. In the morning, it "sunbathes" for a while to help boost its body back up to full operating temperature. To hasten this process, the bird fluffs up the feathers covering its back so that the sunlight warms its skin more effectively.

SWIFTS

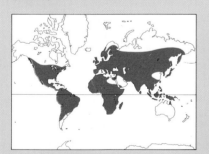

As night falls over a North American city, thousands of small dark birds wheel about in a noisy flock, high above the factory chimneys. At some mysterious signal, the whole flock swoops downwards, disappearing like magic into the darkness of the chimneys. The birds are swifts, and the chimneys provide an artificial alternative to the hollow forest trees that used to be their natural roosting sites.

The Chimney swift of the Americas was forced to change its habits when the ancient forests were cut down to make way for farmland and towns. Its European relative, the Common swift, has also changed its habits. Long ago it nested in caves and on sea-cliffs, but today it is so much a town bird that it is hardly ever seen nesting in "natural" habitats.

MASTERS OF THE AIR

Of all birds, swifts are the most highly specialized for flight. Their long, slender, swept-back wings are designed for fast, gliding flight, high in the air, where they catch most of their insect food. Their legs and feet are weak compared with those of most other birds. They are designed for clinging to the steep walls of their nesting places and not for walking or hopping.

The Common swift of Europe spends almost its entire life in the air. It feeds, sleeps and mates on the wing, and it may remain airborne from the time it leaves the nest until it mates for

---

SWIFTS Apodidae (*71 species*), Hemiprocnidae (Crested swifts: *3 species*)

○ ■ 🐾

Habitat: mainly aerial; nesting in woodland, caves, towns.

Diet: flying insects, especially flies and moths; spiders drifting in the air.

○ Breeding: 1-6 eggs (Crested swifts 1); incubation 17-28 days. Nestling period 34-72 days.

Size: swifts: length 4-12in; weight ⅓-5 ounces. Crested swifts: length 7-13in; weight 2-4 ounces.

Plumage: mainly black or brown, often with white markings. Crested swifts paler, with white stripes on sides of head and prominent crest on top.

Species mentioned in text:
Cave swiftlets (*Collocalia* species)
Chimney swift (*Chaetura pelagica*)
Common swift (*Apus apus*)
Northern white-rumped or Fork-tailed swift (*A. pacificus*)

◄▼Swifts and swiftlets A Seychelles cave swiftlet (*Collocalia elaphra*) **(1)**, now listed as endangered. Common swifts **(2)** mating in flight. An African palm swift (*Cypsiurus parvus*) **(3)**, which glues its nest underneath a palm leaf. An Alpine swift (*Apus melba*) **(4)**, chasing an insect. A Crested tree swift (*Hemiprocne longipennis*) **(5)** of Southeast Asia, incubating its egg on a tiny nest glued to a tree branch.

the first time – two summers later! In this period it may have covered up to 310,000 miles of non-stop flight.

A swift's bill is very broad, and it can be opened wide in order to scoop insects out of the air in flight. The bird's eyes are protected by "eyebrows" of stiff bristles. In the breeding season, the nestlings are fed on balls of insect food, which the parents collect and carry back to the nest in their throats.

SPECIALIST NEST-BUILDERS

Many swifts build cup-shaped nests of feathers, seeds and bits of grass, which they collect high in the air. They cement these items in place with their sticky glue-like saliva. The Cave swiftlets of Asia go one better. They make their nests entirely of saliva, swooping up to the wall of a cave time after time, each time adding a strand of quick-drying saliva to the tiny cup.

▶A Northern white-rumped swift of Asia. Like all swifts, it is agile in flight, but clumsy and awkward on the ground.

SWALLOWS

Darting through the air on a warm summer day, an adult Barn swallow snaps up a bluebottle, then two large hoverflies. In just a few minutes it catches several more flying insects, squashing them into a ball of food which it carries back to its hungry chicks. In a single day a pair of swallows may make up to 400 hunting trips and catch up to 8,000 insects between them!

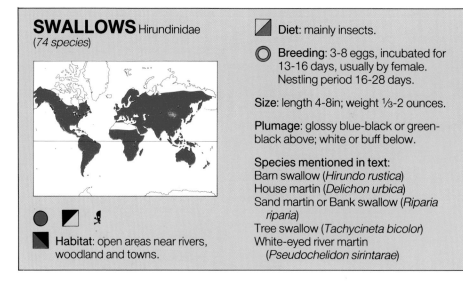

SWALLOWS Hirundinidae
(*74 species*)

● ◨ ☠

◼ **Habitat:** open areas near rivers, woodland and towns.

◨ **Diet:** mainly insects.

◉ **Breeding:** 3-8 eggs, incubated for 13-16 days, usually by female. Nestling period 16-28 days.

Size: length 4-8in; weight ⅓-2 ounces.

Plumage: glossy blue-black or green-black above; white or buff below.

Species mentioned in text:
Barn swallow (*Hirundo rustica*)
House martin (*Delichon urbica*)
Sand martin or Bank swallow (*Riparia riparia*)
Tree swallow (*Tachycineta bicolor*)
White-eyed river martin (*Pseudochelidon sirintarae*)

All swallows are insect-eaters, and their skill at catching insect prey makes them popular with people everywhere. Most of them feed on nothing but insects, though the Tree swallow of North and Central America also eats seeds and berries, especially the fruits of the bayberry tree. The tree provides it with food in cold weather, when insects are scarce.

Each of the 74 different species has its own favorite food insects and its own methods of catching its prey. The New World martins are the biggest members of the family. They feed mainly on moths, butterflies and dragonflies. Smaller species, like the House martin of Europe, catch smaller insects, including greenfly, gnats and midges.

Different swallow species are often able to live together in a fairly small area by concentrating on different prey and by using different feeding behaviors. In warmer weather, for example, the House martin feeds high in the sky while the Barn swallow swoops low across damp meadows, streams and lakes where insects are most plentiful.

WINTER IN THE SUN
For tropical swallows, food supply is seldom a problem. There are plenty of insects available all the year round. For the swallows of the temperate regions, however, life is not so easy. There are very few flying insects around in winter, so the birds are forced to migrate.

Most of Europe's swallows migrate to southern Africa for the winter. Those that inhabit northern North America head for the warmer southern states and Central America. For the European birds, the annual journey is particularly dangerous. To reach their winter quarters the birds must fly across the vast Sahara Desert. The chances of both members of a pair getting there and back again safely are only about one in five. Swallows are often so exhausted by the desert crossing that you can pick them off the twigs where they are resting.

◀Barn swallow chicks showing the huge gape that will later make them such efficient flying insect-catchers.

▲A pair of Sand martins at the entrance to their nest burrow. The 3ft-long burrow probably took 3 to 4 days to dig.

▼A Barn swallow shows off its flying skills by swooping low over a pond and taking a drink without stopping.

HOME AGAIN IN SPRING

European swallows return to their breeding areas between March and June, and their arrival is considered to be the first sign of summer.

Adult birds head straight for their old nesting places. Species such as the Barn swallow and House martin immediately set about repairing the nests they used the previous year. They swoop down to any convenient pool or river bank and collect balls of mud, which they use to reinforce their nests of mud and straw. The Barn swallow builds a simple open cup-shaped nest, stuck to a fence-post or tucked under the eaves of a building. The House martin makes an enclosed nest with a tunnel entrance, and lines it with grass and feathers.

Their close relative the Bank swallow (in Europe known as the Sand martin) uses a different method. The adult birds dig tunnels in steep river banks. The tunnels sometimes collapse during the winter so the birds build a fresh one each year.

Swallows lay their eggs as soon as insect food is in good supply, and once they have hatched, both parents share the task of feeding the hungry chicks. In good summers, a pair of swallows may produce a second family (and even a third) once their first chicks are big enough to look after themselves.

FOUND THEN LOST

Many swallows benefit from living close to people. Buildings provide excellent nest sites, and farmland provides the open hunting habitat the birds like. But there are drawbacks. Farm chemicals and industrial pollution can sometimes reduce the amount of insect food available.

Little is known about some of the tropical swallows, but four species are listed as endangered, including the White-eyed river martin of Thailand. The bird was only discovered in 1968 and has not been seen at all since 1980.

NIGHTJARS

In an experiment, a Common nighthawk was released in a darkened tunnel festooned with ropes. The bird flew through the maze without once colliding with the ropes. Then the test was tried again, but with the bird's ears covered. The nighthawk was unable to find its way through. The ear-muffs had robbed it of its "secret sensor."

The nightjar family is divided into two groups: the nighthawks of North and South America, and the nightjars, which are found in Europe, Asia and Africa as well as in the Americas. Like the Common nighthawk, many species hunt at night using echo-location to find their prey. As with most specialist insect-hunters they are commonest in tropical regions where insects are available all year round. But many species migrate into temperate regions in the summer months.

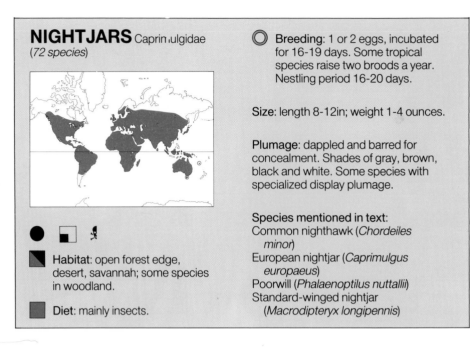

NIGHTJARS Caprinulgidae
(*72 species*)

○ Breeding: 1 or 2 eggs, incubated for 16-19 days. Some tropical species raise two broods a year. Nestling period 16-20 days.

Size: length 8-12in; weight 1-4 ounces.

Plumage: dappled and barred for concealment. Shades of gray, brown, black and white. Some species with specialized display plumage.

Species mentioned in text:
Common nighthawk (*Chordeiles minor*)
European nightjar (*Caprimulgus europaeus*)
Poorwill (*Phalaenoptilus nuttallii*)
Standard-winged nightjar (*Macrodipteryx longipennis*)

● ▣ ⚰

▨ Habitat: open forest edge, desert, savannah; some species in woodland.

▰ Diet: mainly insects.

THE GHOSTLY HUNTERS

The nightjars and nighthawks are true specialists. During the day they rest on the forest floor, or perched on branches, or among the stones and dry scrub of a savannah or desert region. Their patterned plumage of black, brown, gray and white blends into the background so well that the birds are almost impossible to see unless they are disturbed and forced to move.

▶ A European nightjar shows its dappled camouflage plumage as it raises its wings in an angry threat display on its nest on the ground.

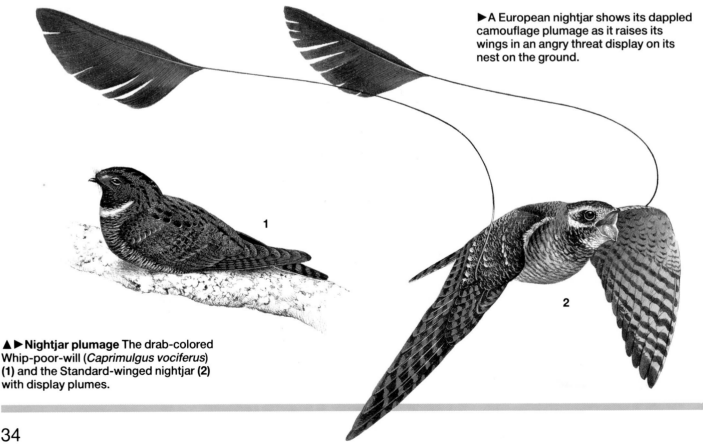

▲ ▶ **Nightjar plumage** The drab-colored Whip-poor-will (*Caprimulgus vociferus*) (**1**) and the Standard-winged nightjar (**2**) with display plumes.

As night falls, the birds become active. Their soft plumage makes hardly a sound as they start to hunt, bobbing and weaving in a graceful dancing flight that makes them look like large moths. There is nothing so charming about the nightjar's mouth. It is enormous! When a nightjar opens its bill wide it becomes a gaping cavern that can take in a cloud of mosquitoes or a huge tropical moth in one gulp. Some of the larger species will even snap up a small night-flying bird if the chance comes along.

Most nightjars remain in flight all the time they are hunting, but some woodland species hunt from a perch, dashing out to snap up a passing insect then returning once more to their look-out.

TUMBLERS AND FLAG-WAVERS
The males of some nightjar species perform spectacular courtship displays to attract their mates. Some involve diving and tumbling display flights. Others make use of long specialized display feathers that are grown just for the mating season. The male may have several females, each with her own nest, and throughout the mating season he must be constantly on guard to chase away other males. Elaborate display plumes are a hindrance to a bird caring for young in the nest, so the males tend to leave care of the young to the females.

"THE SLEEPING ONE"
In 1946 an astonishing discovery was made about a small American nightjar called the poorwill. The bird inhabits the deserts of Mexico and California, and during the winter a bird was found hidden in a crack in the wall of a canyon. The scientists were puzzled by its condition. Its body temperature was well below normal and it was barely breathing, but it was alive. The bird was hibernating – something no other bird has been found to do. The local Hopi Indians had chosen well when they named the bird "Holchko" meaning The Sleeping One.

▲ **Nightjars in display** The Common nighthawk male dives towards the female (1), swooping upwards at the last moment with a booming sound made by the air rushing through specialized feathers. The male Standard-wing nightjar flutters round his chosen mate (2), displaying his 18in-long plumes.

KINGFISHERS

At dusk in the woodlands of eastern Australia, the evening quiet is suddenly shattered by a harsh outburst of hysterical laughter. To an unwary visitor it can be a frightening sound, but this is not the cry of a devil or monster as the early settlers believed. It is the call of a kingfisher – the famous kookaburra, also known as the Laughing jackass.

The strange case of the Laughing jackass is the first hint that the kingfisher family is not quite what many people expect it to be. There are well over 80 different species and they are found in almost every habitat. Some species do feed mainly on fish, but many others inhabit areas far from open water and live by hunting insects and other small animals.

The most primitive types are forest-dwellers that feed on the insects of the forest floor. More specialized kingfishers plunge into water from a perch or from hovering flight to catch fish in rivers, lakes and seas. Others dash from a perch to catch insects in flight, or dig among fallen leaves for worms. Some of the larger species prey on lizards, snakes, crabs and small birds.

Each kind of kingfisher has a bill to suit its hunting style and its prey. One of the oddest-looking species is the Shovel-billed kingfisher of New Guinea. It has a short, wide, cone-shaped bill, which it uses to dig for earthworms. The fish-catchers have long, pointed, dagger-like bills, flattened from side to side. The birds that feed on insects, reptiles, crabs and other prey usually have broad bills, flattened top to bottom.

▼ A European kingfisher returning to its nest hole with a fish. Each of its young may eat 15 fish a day, so the parents may have to catch up to 100 fish every day to feed their brood.

KINGFISHERS Alcedinidae
(86 species)

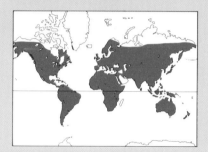

● ◨ ⚐

◨ Habitat: rivers, lakes, coasts; also forest, woodland, savannah and desert.

■ Diet: insects, worms, fish, crabs, lizards and small birds.

○ Breeding: 2 or 3 eggs in tropics; up to 10 in temperate areas. Incubation period 18-22 days, nestling period 20-30 days.

Size: length 4-18in; weight ¼-17 ounces.

Plumage: often colorful. Brilliant blue above, red below. Also greens, browns, black and white.

Species mentioned in text:
European kingfisher (*Alcedo atthis*)
Kookaburra (*Dacelo gigas*)
Shovel-billed kingfisher (*Clytoceyx rex*)
Tuamotu kingfisher (*Halcyon gambieri*)

EUROPE'S FLYING JEWEL

Kingfishers are colorful birds and the European species is among the most beautiful, with its electric-blue back, warm chestnut-orange underparts, bright red legs and jet-black bill. Yet it is very shy, and is surprisingly hard to see until it bursts into action.

This kingfisher usually hunts from a tree perch on the river bank. It takes a variety of small fish, and carries them back to the perch to feed. Most fish are swallowed head-first without delay, but ones with spines – such as sticklebacks – are first beaten against a branch, for only when they are dead will the stiff spines and fins lie flat.

Europe's kingfishers are year-round residents. Courtship starts early in the year with high-flying aerial displays. The pair then dig a nest burrow up to about 3ft deep in the river bank. Up to seven eggs are laid in early May, and once they have hatched, the nest chamber soon becomes overcrowded.

Young kingfishers start trying to fish soon after they leave the burrow, but the learning period can be a dangerous time. Many juvenile kingfishers drown because they dive too often without drying off between dives, and their feathers become waterlogged.

THREATENED SPECIES

The biggest threats to kingfishers are the pollution of rivers and the destruction of tropical forests. Several tropical species are now extremely rare, and at least one has become extinct in the last 70 years. The Tuamotu kingfisher was last seen on the Pacific island of Mangareva in about 1922.

◄**Four of the world's kingfishers** The Pied kingfisher (*Ceryle rudis*) **(1)** of Asia. The Blue-breasted kingfisher *(Halcyon malimbica)* **(2)** of Africa. The Belted kingfisher (*Megaceryle alcyon*) **(3)** of North America, with crest raised. The Amazon kingfisher *(Chloroceryle amazona)* **(4)** of Mexico and Central America.

BEE-EATERS

Perched on a branch of an olive tree in Italy, a brightly colored bird watches a big honeybee moving towards it. In a flash of color, the bird bursts into flight, catching the bee and swooping back to its perch in a graceful upward glide. Banging the bee violently against the side of the branch, the bird stuns it and quickly removes its sting. Then it eats its insect prey.

The bee-eaters are a small family of mainly tropical birds, and they must surely be among the most specialized of all insect-catchers. Their main food consists of honeybees, and they prefer these particular insects to all others, even when they have a choice. What is even more surprising is that most of the bees they catch are the highly poisonous stinging worker bees. Very few of the harmless drones are taken, even when these do stray from the hive and are an easy catch.

To birds with an average weight of only 1½ ounces, a single sting from a large tropical bee could be fatal. The bee-eaters get round this problem in two ways. Firstly, they seem to have a certain amount of natural immunity to the bee's powerful sting (although occasionally they do get badly stung). Secondly, the birds are able to tell the difference between the dangerous species and harmless ones, and they deal with the stinging species very effectively indeed.

A bee-eater attacks from its perch high in a tree or on a fence or telegraph wire, snapping up its prey in a swooping attack or taking it after a short twisting chase in the air. As soon as it gets back to its perch, the bird tosses the insect to the tip of its bill, adjusts its grip, and then stuns the bee by striking it hard against the branch. It then rubs the rear part of the bee's body against the rough bark, which tears away the sharp sting and the poison sacs attached to it. Once the bee has been disarmed in this way, it is swallowed whole.

► A European bee-eater with a cicada in its bill. In the breeding season, the bird will catch up to 225 bees and other insects each day to feed itself and its young.

BEE-EATERS Meropidae
(24 species)

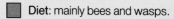

● ◪

◩ **Habitat:** mainly open country, including savannah, steppe, woodland; 6 species in rain forest.

▪ **Diet:** mainly bees and wasps.

○ **Breeding:** 2-4 eggs in tropics; up to 7 in Eurasia. Incubated for 18-23 days, nestling period 27-32 days. Nest burrow up to 10ft long.

Size: length 7-14in; weight ½-2½ ounces.

Plumage: mainly green above, reddish or buff below. Some species black or blue. Males may be brighter than females, with longer tail streamers.

Species mentioned in text:
Carmine bee-eater (*Merops rubicus*)
European bee-eater (*M. apiaster*)
Rainbowbird (*M. ornatus*)
Red-throated bee-eater (*M. bullocki*)
White-throated bee-eater (*M. albicollis*)

39

COLORFUL TRAVELERS

The bee-eater family is spread across the southern part of Europe, the whole of Africa, and through Southeast Asia to New Guinea and Australia. Many species are found in the rain forests of Asia, and it is likely that this is where the family originally came from millions of years ago.

The birds are all brightly colored. Most are green above and reddish below, although one species is mainly black, another pink and gray, and one is deep pink with a green cap. Many species have long central tail feathers, and all have a distinct jet-black eye-mask that gives them a slightly pirate-like appearance.

Forest-dwelling species of bee-eater have rounded wings, but those that live in open country – the African savannah, for example – have long pointed wings. This wing-shape is also typical of species such as the European bee-eater, which migrates far into the temperate regions in the breeding season. At close quarters this species is especially colorful, but even when it flies so high that it is invisible against the blue summer sky, it can still be identified by its rolling "quilp" calls. It is a familiar summer visitor to Spain, Italy and the countries around the eastern end of the Mediterranean Sea. It never strays into the cooler parts of north-west Europe.

BANK BURROWERS

Like their relatives the kingfishers, bee-eaters nest in burrows excavated in soft soil. Some, such as the Red-throated bee-eater of central Africa, will nest only in steep banks. Most members of the family will also dig their burrows sloping down into flat ground if there are no suitable banks available.

◀A colony of Carmine bee-eaters in South Africa. There are two distinct races: this is the southern race, which lacks the greenish-blue throat of the northern race.

The bee-eater's burrow ends in an oval nest chamber. There is no proper nest, or nest-lining, and the eggs are simply laid on the bare earth. Also like the kingfishers, the bee-eaters feed their young in the nest burrow and it quickly becomes half-filled with droppings and the pellets of undigestible food remains coughed up by the birds. A large colony has a smell of ammonia that carries many yards.

FAMILIES AND HELPERS

At the end of its first year, a young bee-eater may find a mate and breed. However, it is more likely to attach itself to an older breeding pair and spend its first season acting as a helper as they raise a family. (This kind of behavior is common among other tropical birds.)

Bee-eater courtship is a simple affair in most species. The male bird chases away any rival males, and often presents the female with small gifts of food. Apart from this there is little ceremony, and the pair quickly set about nesting. One exception is the White-throated bee-eater from East Africa. This has a courtship "butterfly flight," when it flies with wings raised high and slow wing-beats.

The bee-eater pair and any helpers they have share the work of digging the nest burrow, and later of catching food for the nestlings. The chicks remain in the burrow for about 4 weeks, and during this time the entire group roosts in the nest burrow at night. However, soon after the young are able to fly, the group abandons the stinking burrow and thereafter roosts in nearby trees.

In some species, several families and their helpers form special units called clans, and a colony may consist of up to six clans, all living close together. Colonies of Red-throated bee-eaters, for example, may consist of up to 150 birds in nest holes occupying only 1sq yd of cliff face.

▶The rainbowbird is an Australian bee-eater that migrates to Indonesia each year to breed.

▼Bee-eaters in action A Carmine bee-eater **(1)** hitching a ride on an Arabian bustard. A European bee-eater **(2)** hunting. A Blue-cheeked bee-eater (*Merops persicus*) **(3)** snatching a bee from below. A rainbowbird **(4)** with its catch. A Swallow-tailed bee-eater (*M. hirundineus*) **(5)** rubbing a bee against its perch to remove the sting.

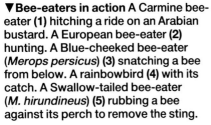

HOOPOE

An eagle flying over a hoopoe's nest fails to see the nestlings until one of them opens its colorful wings to preen. The eagle swoops down to attack. As it approaches, the young birds flutter their wings, both to dazzle the eagle and to strike it should it pounce. The eagle turns tail.

▶An adult hoopoe flattens itself against the ground and points its bill skywards to poke at an attacker from above.

▼A hoopoe bringing food to its brood. When the bird lands, it briefly flicks its crest upright then lowers it again.

HOOPOE *Upupa epops*

● ■

■ **Habitat:** open woodland, farm-land and savannah.

■ **Diet:** insects and lizards.

◎ **Breeding:** 2-5 eggs in tropical regions; 7-9 in temperate regions. Incubated for 15 or 16 days, nestling period 28 days.

Size: length 9-10in; weight 1¾-3 ounces.

Plumage: pinkish-brown with black and white bars; South African race redder, with less white on wings. Plumage the same on males, females and juveniles.

The hoopoe's pinkish-brown plumage and dramatic black-and-white wing bars are very unmistakable, but they are also part of this unusual bird's defenses. When it is feeding quietly on the ground in a field or woodland clearing, the hoopoe is surprisingly difficult to see. It will often remain unnoticed until it opens its wings to fly. When danger threatens, the dazzling pattern of bars on its long tail and short broad wings helps to confuse the attacker as the hoopoe dashes for the safety of trees or scrub vegetation.

BIRD OF THREE CONTINENTS

The hoopoe is found right across southern Europe, all over Africa (apart from the dense tropical rain forest) and throughout southern Asia. It is such a popular and familiar sight that it crops up again and again in the folklore and legends of many lands.

It feeds on the grubs and adults of insects such as grasshoppers and beetles, and on snails. It probes in the grass and soil with its long slender bill, or searches among the cracks and crevices of tree bark or stone walls. In the southern parts of its range it also catches small lizards. These are an important source of food in the breeding season when the bird has hungry youngsters to feed.

The hoopoe's nest site is always a hole of some kind – in a tree or wall, or among rocks. African hoopoes often use holes in termite mounds, or abandoned woodpecker holes. There is no attempt to build a proper nest, and the eggs are simply laid on the bare floor of the nest hole. The female hoopoe incubates the eggs alone, but is kept supplied with food by her attentive mate. She does not leave the nest hole until the young are

▲ The striking bars on the hoopoe's back, wings and tail help to confuse a chasing bird. The bars have the same effect as camouflage patterns painted on military aircraft.

big enough to survive without the warmth of her body. By that time the hole is usually fouled with droppings and the characteristic strong smell of the birds themselves.

The young hoopoes have several ways of defending themselves. If danger threatens, they hiss, stab upwards with their bills, strike out with their wings and squirt their droppings at the intruder.

The bird's common name, hoopoe, and its scientific name, *Upupa epops*, both have the sound of its call – a soft "oop...oop...oop," which carries far and wide through its open habitat.

WOODPECKERS

In the mixed woodlands of the eastern USA, a small black-and-white bird with a red forehead and throat is flitting busily from tree to tree. It drills neat rows of small holes in the bark of each one. The bird is a sapsucker, one of North America's highly specialized woodpeckers. Soon it will return to feed on the sugar-rich sap oozing from the holes, and on the insects that will have gathered there.

The sapsuckers are just one small group in a large and successful family of birds. Woodpecker species are found in most parts of the world. The majority of the birds live in woodlands and forests of various kinds, but some are also found in open grasslands and even in the hottest deserts. A North American species, for example, makes its home in holes in the giant "organ-pipe" cacti that dot the desert landscape of the south-western states.

ENGINEERING MARVELS
Woodpeckers are small- to medium-sized birds with powerful stocky bodies. They have bills designed for hacking and chiseling into dead or decaying wood so they can get at the grubs inside. The design of the neck and skull is a marvel of natural engineering. Somehow it protects the woodpecker's brain from damage despite the jolting and jarring caused by the bird's feeding method. In the case of the Black woodpecker, this can

WOODPECKERS Picidae
(*200 species*)

● ■ ♫

▲ Habitat: tropical, deciduous and coniferous forest; also orchards, parkland, grassland and desert.

▨ Diet: insects, spiders, berries, seeds and tree sap.

◎ Breeding: true woodpeckers: 3-11 eggs, incubated 9-20 days, nestling period 18-35 days. Wrynecks: 5-14 eggs, incubated 12-13 days. Piculets: 2-4 eggs, incubated 11-14 days.

Size: smallest (Scaled piculet): length 3in, weight ¼ ounce; largest (Imperial woodpecker): length 22in, weight 1¼lb.

Plumage: main colors black and white, brown and green, to match habitat. Often with red patches on head.

Species mentioned in text:
Acorn woodpecker (*Melanerpes formicivorus*)
Black woodpecker (*Dryocopus martius*)
European green woodpecker (*Picus viridis*)
Imperial woodpecker (*Campephilus imperialis*)
Sapsuckers (genus *Sphyrapicus*)
Scaled piculet (*Picumnus squamulatus*)
Three-toed woodpecker (*Picoides tridactylus*)

▼ ▶ A group of woodpeckers Three-toed woodpecker (1). Common flicker (*Colaptes auratus*) (2). Green woodpecker (3). Olive-backed three-toed woodpecker (*Dinopium rafflesi*) (4). Northern wryneck (*Jynx torquilla*) (5). Great spotted woodpecker (*Picoides major*) (6). Red-headed woodpecker (*Melanerpes erythrocephalus*) (7). Pileated woodpecker (*Dryocopus pileatus*) (8). Yellow-bellied sapsucker (*Sphyrapicus varius*) (9).

45

mean cushioning the shock of up to 12,000 hammer blows each day.

The woodpecker's feet have two toes facing forward and two facing back. Each toe ends in a sharp claw, and the fourth toe on each foot can be turned out sideways so that the bird can vary its grip to cope with any shape or angle of branch.

Even the tail of a woodpecker is special. The feathers have extra strong, stiff shafts, and when the tail is pressed against the tree trunk it both supports the bird and acts like a spring to absorb the shock of the hammering.

FEEDING VARIATIONS

Most woodpeckers feed mainly on insects such as beetles and ants and their grubs, and on spiders. Some of this food is simply picked off the surface of the bark, or pecked out of the cracks. Some is found by prying up large flakes of loose bark.

The Three-toed woodpecker drills small round holes in the tree bark then pokes its long pointed tongue inside to "harpoon" the tasty grubs. Other species have sticky tips to their tongues.

Even average-sized species like the Black woodpecker of Europe can do a surprising amount of damage to a tree. Holes 20in high, 6in wide and up to 5in deep are often hacked in soft-wooded trees such as larch as the bird searches for its favorite food – Hercules ants.

Most woodpeckers vary their diet with seeds, fruits, nuts and berries, and some species even specialize on plant food. The Acorn woodpecker of North and South America feeds almost entirely on acorns, which it stores for the winter in holes specially excavated in a "larder tree." One tree, used by a small party of six Acorn woodpeckers, was found to contain more than 50,000 storage holes! In Europe, the Great spotted woodpecker often carries pine cones to a favorite feeding tree and wedges them into cracks in the bark while it pecks out the fatty seeds.

The majority of woodpeckers can extend their tongue far beyond the end of the bill (up to 4in beyond in

▲**Woodpecker feeding methods** The simplest technique (1), gleaning ants and other insects from the bark surface. Using the long tongue (2) to extract grubs from holes drilled in the wood.

◀A male Great spotted woodpecker launches itself from the nest-hole at the start of a hunting trip. Once the chicks are able to fly, each parent will look after half the brood until they are able to fend for themselves.

the case of the European green woodpecker), but the sapsuckers cannot do this. So, instead of excavating deep holes and fishing out grubs and adult insects with their tongues, the sapsuckers drill their shallow holes in the bark and wait for their food to come to them! They lick up the sticky droplets of tree sap with the tip of the tongue, which is fringed with fine bristles rather like a brush.

FAMILY LIFE
Most woodpeckers remain in the same area throughout the year, living in territories "owned" by single birds or by pairs or family groups. By claiming a territory, and defending it against intruders, the birds make sure

they have a good supply of food, plenty of sheltered roosting places, and at least a few old trees that will provide holes for nesting. Acorn woodpeckers have large family territories occupied by up to 15 related birds. With so many helpers on call, the family has no difficulty protecting its acorn stores against raiders.

Woodpeckers have a complicated "language" of signs and sounds. The birds communicate with one another by ruffling the feathers on their head and by fanning their wings. They also use bobbing and dancing movements and they drum on tree trunks and branches with their bill. Courtship begins with drumming and display flights by both sexes. Each bird uses

these signals to announce that it is ready to mate, or that it has a good nest site available. Other displays are used to warn rivals to stay away.

Newly paired males and females share the work of excavating a nest-hole, and this can take 10 to 28 days according to the species. It is quite a task. More than 10,000 wood chips have been found littering the ground beneath a new Black woodpecker nest-hole. Once they have made a hole, a pair will use it for many years and will not usually create another unless they are pushed out of their original home by jackdaws or starlings. Both the male and female share the work of incubating the eggs, and later of feeding the nestlings.

LYREBIRDS

A male Superb lyrebird sweeps its long tail feathers up and forwards over its back in a shimmering cascade of silver and white. The bird pours out loud musical song and slowly turns around. Soon a female arrives, attracted by the song.

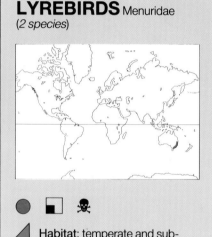

LYREBIRDS Menuridae
(2 species)

● ◼ ☠

△ Habitat: temperate and sub-tropical rain forest.

◼ Diet: earthworms, and adult insects and grubs in soil and dead wood.

◯ Breeding: 1 egg, incubated by female for about 50 days; nestling period about 47 days.

Size: males: length 36-40in, weight up to 2½lb; females: length 30-35in, weight up to 2lb.

Plumage: brown above; buff to gray-brown underneath. Mature males have long tail plumes; female's tail is short.

Species mentioned in text:
Prince Albert's lyrebird (*Menura alberti*)
Superb lyrebird (*M. novaehollandiae*)

▶ A male Superb lyrebird with his tail fanned. Prince Albert's lyrebird lacks the two broad outermost feathers.

Both the Superb lyrebird and the slightly less ornate Prince Albert's lyrebird are found in the temperate and subtropical forests of south-eastern Australia. They are pheasant-sized birds that spend their time on the forest floor, using their long powerful legs to scratch in the earth for worms and insect food.

MOUNDS AND LINED NESTS
Male Superb lyrebirds live for up to 15 years, and they grow their long adult tail feathers during the first 5 to 7 years. Young males wander through the forest in small groups, but as each bird reaches maturity it chooses a home territory of 6½-8½ acres (an acre is about half the area of a soccer field) and settles down. It defends its territory by singing, displaying, and by chasing away intruders.

The male lyrebird then scratches up as many as 20 earth mounds, each about 5ft across. These are its display mounds, and during the breeding season it will spend most of the day walking from one mound to another,

singing and performing its spectacular display dance.

Once it has a female to perform to, the male bird quivers its long display plumes and makes a curious clicking call. It runs from side to side in an arc around the female, then jumps towards her and back again in time with its song. The male ends its display with two loud, ringing, bell-like notes that carry far and wide through the forest.

There are no permanent bonds between male and female lyrebirds. They meet at the display mounds simply in order to mate, and immediately afterwards the female goes off to her nest in her own territory nearby. The male may have several mates, but after mating he plays no further part in raising the family. That is left entirely to the females.

The female lyrebird usually lays a single gray or brown egg in a bulky domed nest made of twigs, moss, bark and fern fronds, lined with feathers and soft vegetation. Generally, she builds the nest low down against an earth bank or the base of a tree, but

▲ In the gloom of the forest, a female Superb lyrebird feeds her young male offspring.

▼ The young lyrebird's droppings are enclosed in a transparent membrane and the female removes them from the nest every day. Often they are thrown into a hole in the ground so they do not attract predators to the nest.

sometimes she nests up to 70ft high among the branches of trees.

LONG-TERM CARE
The lyrebird's egg is unusually resistant to cold, and even in the early stages of incubation it can be left unattended for many hours without coming to harm. If the egg could not

withstand cooling, the female lyrebird would not be able to leave the nest to feed herself. The female's need to abandon the egg for long periods also explains why she builds such a big enclosed nest. It is to help keep the egg (and later the nestling) warm, and to keep it dry when it rains.

The female takes good care of her chick. She feeds it and cares for it in the nest for about 6 weeks after hatching, but the youngster will stay with her for up to 8 months altogether. During that time she continues to feed it.

PROTECTED BEAUTIES
In the last century, lyrebirds were hunted for their tail feathers for the fashion trade, but today they are protected. The main threat they now face is the continuing destruction of their ancient forest habitat.

TYRANT FLYCATCHERS

In 1976 a team of scientists discovered a new species of flycatcher living in the cloud-covered mountain forests of Peru. In 1981 another new species was found, this time in Peru's lowland rain forests. It had remained undiscovered for years because of its tiny size and tree-top life-style. These birds are just two of the most recent additions to the New World's biggest and most varied family of birds, the tyrant flycatchers.

With 376 species listed so far, the tyrant flycatchers are by far the most successful group of birds in the Americas. Some breed as far north as the spruce forests of Canada and others as far south as the tree-less hillsides of Tierra del Fuego. In between, there are flycatchers living in every habitat from the dry grasslands of Argentina to the rain forests of Ecuador and the beaches of the Caribbean. In South America almost one land-bird in every ten is a flycatcher.

CATCHING FOOD IN FLIGHT
The family name "flycatcher" is a little misleading. Some species do feed entirely on insects, but most of them also eat berries. A few also eat fruit, small fish, lizards and snakes. Even among the insect-eaters, there are many different hunting methods.

The most common flycatchers are medium-sized, dull-colored birds that live in tree-tops or along the forest edge. Many have broad bills, fringed with bristles, and they hunt by snatching insects from the leaves of trees during short flights from a favorite perch. Others have slender pointed bills and take most of their food from the tiny cracks and spaces in bark and among foliage. A few species, including the elegant Fork-tailed flycatcher, specialize in catching insects on the

TYRANT FLY-CATCHERS Tyrannidae
(*376 species*)

  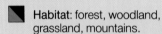

Habitat: forest, woodland, grassland, mountains.

Diet: mainly insects, some fruits; occasionally fish, frogs and lizards.

Breeding: 2-8 eggs (usually 3 or 4), laid in woven nest or in natural or excavated cavity. Incubated for 14-20 days, nestling period 14-23 days.

Size: smallest (pygmy-tyrants): length 2½in, weight ⅛ ounce; largest (shrike-tyrants): length up to 20in, weight up to 3 ounces.

Plumage: mainly dull olive above, pale yellow below; also shades of brown. Some species with bright colors on crown. One species bright red.

Species mentioned in text:
Boat-billed flycatcher
    (*Megarhynchus pitangua*)
Fork-tailed flycatcher (*Muscivora tyrannus*)
Great kiskadee (*Pitangus sulphuratus*)
Ground-tyrants (genus *Muscisaxicola*)
Pygmy-tyrants (6 genera)
Shrike-tyrants (genus *Agriornis*)
Tody-tyrants (genus *Hemitriccus*)
White-bearded flycatcher (*Conopias inornatus*)

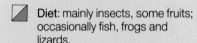

wing. Long outer tail feathers give these birds the extra maneuverability they need to fly in between trees to catch their prey in mid-air.

LIZARD- AND FISH-EATERS
The largest flycatchers are the jay-sized shrike-tyrants that inhabit the high grasslands of the Andes. They scan the ground from a hunting perch, and pounce on large insects and lizards, which they kill with blows from their powerful hook-tipped

bills. Their relatives, the ground-tyrants, have longer legs, and catch their insect prey in fast darting runs, although they too will take to the air to pursue an escaping insect. These larger flycatchers include several eye-catching species with yellow under-parts and black-and-white striped crowns. One of the best-known is the Great kiskadee. It will eat almost anything, but is especially fond of small fish, which it catches in shallow water at the edges of lakes and streams.

At the opposite end of the size-scale are the pygmy-tyrants and the tody-tyrants. Most are green or yellow in color and live in the dense vegetation of the lowlands. Several of these smaller species are among the 16 flycatchers that are now threatened because so much of the forest is being cut down for timber and to make way for agriculture.

FAMILY LIFE

Some flycatchers live alone for most of the year and find a new mate at the start of each new breeding season. Others remain with their mates all year round. The work of incubating the eggs and brooding the young is in most species done by the female, while the male often perches nearby, guarding the territory and the nest site. He will often perch in the same place for hours on end.

Once the chicks are hatched, both parents share the task of feeding them until they become independent a few months later. In some species the young leave to find their own territory almost immediately, but many spend the first year close to their parents. Young White-bearded flycatchers take this one stage further. They stay with their parents for several years and act as helpers as new families are raised each year.

◀▲New World flycatchers A Short-tailed pygmy flycatcher (*Myiornis ecaudata*) (1). A Great kiskadee (2) with its prey. A Fork-tailed flycatcher (3) pursuing a flying insect. A Vermilion flycatcher (*Pyrocephalus rubinus*) (4). A male Royal flycatcher (*Onychorynchus coronatus*) (5) with crest raised in display.

▲The Boat-billed flycatcher inhabits open country, often near water, and feeds on a variety of insects, other invertebrates and on frogs.

PITTAS

For many years the African pitta was thought to spend its whole life in southern Africa. But 50 years ago, a scientist living in distant Tanzania became curious about reports of birds flying into lighted houses during the night. To his surprise he discovered that some of the birds were pittas, and that they always turned up at the same time of year. He had unlocked their secret, for these shy, brightly-colored songbirds are regular night-time migrants.

PITTAS Pittidae (26 species)

Diet: earthworms, snails, adult insects and grubs.

Breeding: 1-7 eggs (usually 3-5) in summer in north and south of range; all year round near equator (except for the monsoon period).

Size: length 6-11in; weight 1½-7 ounces.

Plumage: often brown or green above; splashed with brilliant colors on head and undersides.

Species mentioned in text:
African pitta (*Pitta angolensis*)
Banded pitta (*P. guajana*)
Hooded pitta (*P. sordida*)

Habitat: forest, bamboo jungle, mangroves; also plantations and overgrown gardens.

When scientists came to investigate the movements of pittas in other parts of Africa and Asia they discovered that at least eight species migrate at night. What is even more curious is that the pittas travel during the new Moon, rather than choosing the full Moon like most songbirds.

JEWELS OF THE FOREST
With their short stocky bodies and long legs, the pittas are well equipped for life spent mainly at ground level in the rain forests, bamboo thickets, mangroves and jungles of southern Asia, Africa and northern Australia. What is truly astonishing is their color, for unlike many birds of the dark forest interior, the pittas are adorned with brilliant patches of scarlet, turquoise, yellow and green.

▼ **Pittas feeding** An Indian pitta (*Pitta brachyura*) **(1)** and the rare Gurney's pitta (*P. gurneyi*) **(2)**. The birds feed on worms, insects and snails in the soil and leaf litter of the forest floor. They feed by probing with the bill, and by scratching with their feet.

▲A Hooded pitta removes a sac full of nestlings' droppings from its nest. This cleaning behavior ensures the delicate nest lasts for up to 3 weeks.

If the birds are alarmed, they can become almost invisible by turning their drab brown backs towards the threat and remaining absolutely still. But when they are courting, it is a different matter. The males strut about, bolt upright, bobbing up and down with wings half raised to show off their glorious colors. Then, they are among the most dazzling of all the songbirds.

SHARING THE WORK

Male and female pittas share the work of building the large, untidy nest of twigs and rootlets, which they usually place low in a thicket or by a fallen tree or rock pile. They also share the incubation of the eggs and the feeding of the young, but strangely they often chase the young away soon after they are able to leave the nest. If danger threatens while the young are still in the nest, the adults often try to hide the entrance with a leafy twig, then trick the intruder away from the nest by moving off through the under-growth, calling anxiously.

►The Banded pitta lives in the dark forests of Thailand, western Malaysia and the Greater Sunda Islands.

LARKS

In the Sahara Desert a small but conspicuous bird flies high into the sky. As it spirals upwards, its ringing song carries far and wide. The bird is a male Bifasciated lark in display, inviting females to admire his strength, and warning other males to stay clear of his territory.

LARKS Alaudidae (76 species)

Habitat: any open country.

Diet: seeds, insects, spiders.

Breeding: 2-6 eggs, incubated for 11-16 days. Up to 3 clutches in temperate regions, usually 1 in desert regions.

Size: length 5-10in; weight ½-2½ ounces.

Plumage: mainly brown, with black and white markings. One species (the Black lark) completely black.

Species mentioned in text:
Bifasciated lark (*Alaemon alaudipes*)
Black lark (*Melanocorypha yeltoniensis*)
Desert lark (*Ammomanes deserti*)
Fischer's finch-lark (*Eremopterix leucopareia*)
Flappet lark (*Mirafra rufocinnamomea*)
Horned lark (*Eremophila alpestris*)
Long-clawed lark (*Heteromirafra archeri*)
Thick-billed lark (*Rhamphocoris clotbey*)

▲ The Flappet lark of African savannah regions is one of several lark species that frequently sing from the top of a post, bush or tree.

Most people are familiar with larks through the type of song and display used by the Bifasciated lark. Larks are birds of wide open spaces. They are found in habitats as varied as the Arctic tundra, the cold steppes of Asia and the scrub grasslands of Australia. But nowhere are they as common or as typical as in the deserts and semi-deserts of Africa.

AT HOME IN THE DESERT

In sand deserts (ergs) and rocky deserts (hammadas) a host of these small birds manage to make a living on the sparse food supply of seeds and insects. Small-sized species such as the Desert lark pick up seeds and spiders, and peck at the droppings of larger animals in search of undigested seeds. Larger species like the Bifasciated lark use their stronger bills also to dig ant-lion larvae out of the hot sand.

It is no accident that the main plumage colors in the lark family are soft browns, often with darker brown markings and patches of white. These are the colors of concealment, for the larks are mainly ground-dwelling birds. Their display flights may take them high into the sky, but they feed and nest on the ground, and it is there that they are most in need of protection. For desert-living larks the main danger is from desert foxes and from the swooping low-level attacks of the Lanner falcon. For the Horned lark, which breeds in the Arctic, the threats include stoats, the Peregrine falcon and merlins.

SHARP CLAWS, TOUGH BILLS

Like most ground-dwelling birds, larks have longish legs, and their feet have long, strong toes with sharp claws. The rear-facing fourth toe has a specially long claw that probably helps the bird to balance as it runs across rough ground. A few species take to the air at the first sign of danger, but rather surprisingly many larks prefer to run or even to walk away from danger. They are absolute masters at using every slight dip in the ground, and every stone or plant, to provide cover as they slip away almost as if by magic.

Most larks feed mainly on seeds, but insect food plays an important part in their lives, especially when they are feeding young birds in the nest. In deserts, where there is little vegetation, plant seeds are naturally quite scarce, so insects such as beetles – as well as spiders – are snapped up whenever the chance comes along.

Differences in diet often show up in the bill shapes of different species. The long and slightly down-curved bill of the Bifasciated lark is perfect for digging insects and seeds from the loose sand. Fischer's finch-lark has a short strong pointed bill for dealing with hard seeds and for poking about among stones and vegetation for the occasional insect or spider.

Most extreme of all is the bill of the Thick-billed lark. It is a massive structure, broad and thick like that of the European hawfinch, and quite strong enough to crack the toughest seed-case.

▼A selection of lark species The skylark (*Alauda arvensis*) (1) of Europe and Asia in song flight. The Horned lark (2) of North America, Europe and Asia. Fischer's finch-lark (3) of East Africa. A Singing bush-lark (*Mirafra javanica*) (4) of East Africa, India, South-east Asia and Australia.

NESTS AND NESTLINGS

In the breeding season, many members of the lark family claim territories, and the spectacular display flights and loud songs of the male birds have two purposes: they are an invitation to unattached females looking for mates, and a warning to other males to keep well away.

Most species build simple cup-shaped nests of grass stems which they place on the ground, sometimes partly hidden by vegetation. Desert species often place their nests low down in bushes where the air is a little cooler and the nest is shaded from the Sun. The eggs are usually laid at the start of the rainy season so that seeds and insects are most plentiful at the time the chicks hatch out.

Just how many chicks are raised varies from one habitat to another. In temperate regions a pair of larks may raise two or even three broods in a season, each of 4 to 6 chicks. In hot dry regions, where food is scarce, a pair may have to work hard to raise a single brood of two chicks.

THE RARE ONES

Although the Bifasciated and the Horned larks are not in any danger, some of their relatives are less fortunate. Some species are beginning to suffer from poisoning by farm chemicals. Others are facing food shortages in areas where crop-spraying has removed the weeds that provide their winter supply of seeds.

Rarest and most endangered of all larks are six African species. They include the Long-clawed lark of Somalia whose habitat has been destroyed by farming, cattle-grazing and by drought. It has been seen only once since 1922.

▶A female Horned lark stands over its nest, which it usually scratches out in gravel ridges or on shores. The female is duller than the male, with less prominent horns.

WAGTAILS AND PIPITS

To learn more about bird migration scientists regularly catch large numbers of birds and mark them by putting lightweight colored rings or bands on their legs. Recently, during a ringing session in West Africa, the date-ring on the leg of one European Yellow wagtail showed that it had originally been marked 7 years earlier. In the years between, the bird must have crossed the Sahara Desert at least 14 times!

WAGTAILS AND PIPITS Motacillidae (*54 species*)

○ **Breeding:** 2-7 eggs, incubated by female or both parents for 12-20 days.

Size: length 5-9in; weight ½-1¾ ounces.

Plumage: wagtails: black, white and gray above, yellow below; pipits: mainly brown, often heavily streaked.

Species mentioned in text:
Citrine wagtail (*Motacilla citreola*)
Golden pipit (*Tmetothylacus tenellus*)
Gray wagtail (*Motacilla cinerea*)
Pangani longclaw (*Macronyx aurantigula*)
White wagtail (*Motacilla alba*)
Yellow wagtail (*M. flava*)

● ■ ☠

▨ **Habitat:** open country.

◪ **Diet:** mainly insects; some snails and vegetable food.

▼**Wagtails and pipits** A Yellow wagtail **(1)** holding an insect. This is the black-headed variety found in East Europe and Asia. Richard's pipit (*Anthus novae-seelandiae*) **(2)** is found in Africa, Asia and Australia. The Yellow-throated longclaw (*Macronyx croceus*) **(3)** is an African wagtail.

The wagtails and pipits may not hold any of the long-range migrant records of the bird world, but they are a good example of the amazing journeys that are made every year by many of the familiar songbirds of the Northern Hemisphere.

TRAVELING SONGSTERS

In the fall, Yellow wagtails from Britain usually fatten up for 2 to 3 weeks before leaving their breeding areas. They then fly non-stop to southern Spain or North Africa, pausing there for a brief rest before setting off again to cross the Sahara Desert. Some birds even make the entire 2,500-mile journey to the savannah lands south of the Sahara in one continuous flight lasting more than 70 hours. The few Yellow wagtails that breed in Alaska cross back over the Bering Strait each year and fly south to spend the winter in South-east Asia. There they are joined by millions of their relatives from northern Asia.

Many other wagtails and pipits make shorter journeys, leaving their mountain and moorland summer homes to spend the winter months near the coast.

AN ADAPTABLE FAMILY

Wagtails and pipits are birds of open country. The family probably first evolved in Africa, and even today the savannah grasslands are the main home of the well-known Golden pipit and the eight species of longclaws. The wagtails are more widespread. Some are found only in Africa, but many more are found right across Europe and Asia. They are mainly birds of wet grassland areas, and are most often found close to rivers and lakes. The pipit group, though, has the widest distribution of all. These birds are found mainly in drier country – in grasslands, open woodland and even in semi-desert regions.

One reason why the wagtails and pipits have been so successful is that,

unlike many birds, they have actually benefited from the changes people have made to the landscape. Where forests have been cut down to make way for cultivation, cattle and sheep grazing, towns and villages, the huge new areas of open country have provided more and more living space and feeding opportunities for these birds. Sadly, many other species have suffered in the same process.

CHASERS AND FLYCATCHERS

Most of the wagtails and pipits are small, slender, graceful birds with long legs, extremely long toes, and long thin tails. Like many insect-eaters, they are nimble and agile, and the Gray wagtail, with its constantly flicking tail, is one of the most graceful of all riverside birds.

The longclaws of Africa have fairly stout bills to help deal with the tough-bodied beetles that are their main food. Most other species have long slender bills. Some wagtails and pipits catch their prey with a sudden lunge of the bill as they walk along, or after a short chase. Others take their prey in short flights from a favorite perch.

Different hunting methods seem to go with different body shapes. For example, the Citrine wagtail has long

▲A juvenile White wagtail takes a bath in a pond. In adult plumage it will be white below and gray above, with a black cap and throat.

▼The Pangani longclaw is a member of the genus *Macronyx* (eight species) which are wagtails that inhabit the grasslands, woodlands and marshes of much of Africa.

legs and a short tail. It usually hunts in the shallow waters at the edge of a lake or slow-moving river, picking insects, shrimps and snails from the water and from among the rocks and weeds. By contrast, the Gray wagtail has short legs and a very long tail. It hunts from a rocky perch by a fast-flowing stream, darting out to catch insects flying over the water. The exceptionally long tail acts like a rudder and enables the bird to twist and turn in flight with great precision and agility.

RAISING A FAMILY

Most of the wagtails and pipits build their nests on the ground or low down in a clump of dense vegetation. The nest is usually a deep cup of grass, twigs and leaves, warmly lined with animal hair and feathers. A few species prefer to nest in holes – both natural and artificial. The White wagtail, for example, often nests among the loose rocks of talus slopes, or in holes in stone walls, while the Gray wagtail frequently makes use of riverbank holes and cavities in the brickwork of bridges.

Most of the migrant European species return to their breeding grounds in April. The breeding season, for them and for the year-round resident birds, lasts through May, June and July, when insect food is plentiful.

In some species the female incubates the eggs and feeds the young without any help from her mate. In other species both parents share the work. Second broods are common in many species, especially in years when the weather is warm and the food supply good.

◄A Gray wagtail with a healthy brood of six nestlings. This species is found across Europe and Asia as far east as Japan. It can be found near fast-flowing mountain streams at 6,600ft in the Alps and as high as 13,200ft in Kashmir.

SHRIKES

SHRIKES Laniidae (*70 species*), Campephagidae (*72*), Irenidae (*14*), Prionopidae (*9*), Vangidae (*13*), Bombycillidae (*8*) and Dulidae (*1*)

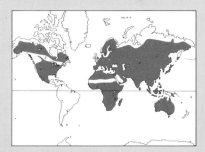

● ◨ ⚕

◨ **Habitat:** tropical forest, dry savannah woodland, cultivated land, coastal scrubland.

◪ **Diet:** mainly insects; larger species take lizards, frogs, birds. Some also eat fruit.

○ **Breeding:** true shrikes usually lay 4-7 eggs; incubation 12-18 days. Other groups vary; details unknown for some.

Size: length 6-15in; weight ⅓-4 ounces. Details unknown for many species.

Plumage: some species mainly black, white and gray, others brightly colored in crimson, yellow, green; often with streaks, spots and blotches.

Species mentioned in text:
Gonoleks (genus *Laniarius*)
Great gray, or Northern, shrike (*Lanius excubitor*)
Helmet shrikes (genus *Prionops*)
Helmet vanga (*Euryceros prevostii*)
Minivets (genus *Pericrocotus*)
Red-backed shrike (*Lanius collurio*)
Red-tailed vanga (*Calicalicus madagascariensis*)

Perched on a fence-post on a New England farm, a Great gray shrike scans the ground for prey. A movement in the grass catches the bird's eye, and like a miniature hawk it pounces. Returning to its perch with a large beetle in its bill, the bird moves out along the fence wire and with a brisk movement of its head impales the beetle on one of the sharp steel barbs.

Many members of the shrike family hunt from a look-out perch in this way, and several species have the "butcher-bird" habit of storing food. These birds impale insects on sharp thorns or, in farming areas, on the spikes of barbed wire fences.

The main prey of the smaller

◄Shrikes and their relatives Large cuckoo-shrike (*Coracina novae-hollandiae*) (1) of India, south Asia and Australia. The Great gray or Northern shrike (2) of North America, Europe, Africa and Asia. Red-shouldered cuckoo-shrike (*Campephaga phoenicia*) (3) of East Africa. The Long-crested helmet-shrike (*Prionops plumata*) (4) from Africa. The Helmet vanga (*Euryceros prevostii*) (5) of Madagascar holding a lizard's tail. A palmchat (*Dulus dominicus*) (6) from Hispaniola, and a Burchell's gonolek (*Laniarius atrococcineus*) (7) of South Africa.

COATS OF MANY COLORS

There are seven families of shrikes and their relatives. The true shrikes (family Laniidae) are the most widespread. As well as being found throughout Africa south of the Sahara Desert, they are also found in Europe and Asia and across most of North America.

Another big family, the cuckoo-shrikes (Campephagidae), lives in the forests and scrublands of southern Africa, South-east Asia and Australia. These birds range from drab-colored forest birds the size of pigeons to dainty and brilliantly colored birds called minivets, which have slender wings and long tails. They are all highly sociable birds, and often move through the tree-tops in noisy bands of 20 or more as they search among the leaves for insects.

The vanga-shrikes, or vangas (family Vangidae), are found only on the huge island of Madagascar. Their ancestors probably belonged to the helmet-shrike family (Prionopidae) of Africa, but for millions of years they have evolved in complete isolation. Madagascar has very few other groups of native birds, and so the vangas have been able to take over many different life-styles. The Helmet vanga preys on large insects, chameleons and frogs – it is like a small bird of prey. The Red-tailed vanga has a small pointed bill and searches the tree bark for small insects, just as a tit does. Other species behave like flycatchers.

shrikes, like the Red-backed shrike of western Europe, consists of bumble-bees, grasshoppers and other large insects. The much more powerful Great gray shrike often takes mice, lizards and even young birds, which are snatched from the nest while the parents are away gathering food.

Three-quarters of the shrike species are found in Africa. Some inhabit rain forests, others deciduous woodlands or savannah country. Many species are brightly colored, for example the spectacular gonoleks, but all have the powerful hook-tipped bill that is the main family characteristic.

MOCKINGBIRDS

The rare Puerto Rican parrot faces a double threat. While foresters are cutting down the tall trees it needs for nesting, Pearly-eyed thrashers – West Indian relatives of the North American mockingbirds – are stealing its eggs and young, and driving it away from its few remaining nest sites.

MOCKINGBIRDS
Mimidae (*30 species*)

● ◪

◪ Habitat: scrub and woodland.

◪ Diet: insects, worms, spiders, fruit; some species take birds' eggs.

○ Breeding: usually 2-5 eggs, incubated for 12-13 days.

Size: length 8-12in; weight about 2 ounces.

Plumage: brown or gray above, paler below, usually with darker streaks.

Species mentioned in text:
Brown thrasher (*Toxostoma rufum*)
Catbird (*Dumetella carolinensis*)
Curve-billed thrasher (*Toxostoma curvirostre*)
Galapagos mockingbird (*Nesomimus trifasciatus*)
Northern mockingbird (*Mimus polyglottos*)
Patagonian mockingbird (*M. patagonicus*)
Pearly-eyed thrasher (*Margarops fuscatus*)
Sage thrasher (*Toxostoma montanus*)

The behavior of the thrashers illustrates two of the main characteristics of the mockingbird family. Although not big birds, most of them are tough and aggressive, especially during the breeding season. They also take a wide range of different foods, and the larger species do not hesitate to rob the nests of other birds.

AMERICA'S TALENTED MIMICS
The mockingbirds are a New World family related to the thrushes and wrens. They are about the same size as thrushes, and rather similar in color and markings, but they have longer bills and tails.

Their family name comes from their skill as mimics. Their own songs are loud and clear and carry for great distances, but many species can also copy the calls and songs of other birds living in the same habitats. Mockingbirds use this skill very effectively when defending their territories. As well as chasing away birds of their own species, mockingbirds will chase away birds of other species too – often by imitating the sounds of angry resident male birds. Their talent also includes mimicking non-bird sounds. Mockingbirds have been heard imitating squeaky gates, cars, frogs, musical instruments and even human voices.

RESIDENTS AND MIGRANTS
Mockingbirds are found exclusively in the Americas, from the southern part of Canada south through the USA and Central America to southern Chile. They are, however, mainly birds of the warmer regions. Only the catbird and the Brown thrasher live as far north as Canada, while the Patagonian mockingbird is the only one found in southern Argentina and Chile.

Birds of the warm tropical zone remain in their home ranges all the year round, but most of the northern birds migrate in winter. The Canadian catbirds and thrashers fly south to the southern states and Central America. Even the Sage thrasher leaves its home in the dry sagebrush plains of western North America to spend the winter in New Mexico and Texas.

▼ The Curve-billed thrasher of Arizona, Texas and Mexico usually builds its nest in a fork in a cholla cactus.

CRAB- AND EGG-EATERS

The mockingbirds' main habitats are scrubland and the lower levels of woodland vegetation, though many species inhabit dry semi-desert areas. The two main exceptions are one species that lives in dense rain forest on the island of Dominica, and one that inhabits dense marshland vegetation across a large part of northern South America.

The birds' main food consists of insect grubs and adults, worms and spiders which are dug out of the ground or from the leaf litter. Fruits and berries are also eaten whenever they are available. The Galapagos mockingbird preys on small crabs along the shoreline, and like the Pearly-eyed thrasher it is also a well-known nest robber, taking the eggs of many of the islands' sea-birds and land-birds.

SOCIAL LIFE

Many of the mockingbirds live alone for most of the year, some stay together in pairs, and in just a few species the birds live in small groups of up to 10 birds. In these groups, the breeding pair are often assisted by the other birds, some of which may be their own young from earlier broods.

The eggs are highly variable in color. In some species they are white, in others dark greenish-blue, often with dark streaks or spots. They are laid in a large, untidy, cup-shaped nest of grass and twigs, usually placed on the ground or low down in a bush. During the breeding season, some mockingbirds become aggressive and will even attack dogs that approach too near their nest-site.

▶The Northern mockingbird is one of the finest mimics in the family although like most mockingbirds its copy-cat calls make up only about one-tenth of its total vocal output. It is widespread across most of the USA.

WRENS

Starting about 9,000 years ago, each spring a few small brown birds flew across the Bering Strait from the New World into the Old in search of breeding areas and mates. These were Common wrens, known in the USA as Winter wrens, and since that time this species of tiny bird has spread across Asia and throughout western Europe.

WRENS Troglodytidae
(*59 species*)

● ◨ 🐾

◨ **Habitat**: dense undergrowth in forest, woodland and gardens. Some species in semi-desert areas.

■ **Diet**: insects, (especially grubs, butterflies and moths) and spiders.

○ **Breeding**: temperate species up to 10 eggs, tropical species 2-4; incubation 12-20 days.

Size: length of most species 3-5in, weight 1/3-1/2 ounce; Cactus wren 6½-9in.

Plumage: brown, sometimes with yellow or reddish tinge; darker barring on back, paler below, sometimes spotted.

Species mentioned in text:
Cactus wren (*Campylorhynchus brunneicapillus*)
Common or Winter wren (*Troglodytes troglodytes*)
Musician wren (*Cyphorhinus aradus*)

The beginning of spring marks the start of a 3-month period of almost non-stop activity for the male Common wren. Like several of his North American relatives, he will court and mate with more than one female (usually two and sometimes three). To attract his mates he first builds several nests in his territory. He may have 3 or 4 ready for use at any time, but over the full season may build as many as 12. (North American marsh wrens may build 35 nests in a season!)

When a female enters the territory – attracted by the male's loud and cheerful song – he leads her straight to a nest with a fluttering display flight. He then invites her inside by repeatedly bobbing in and out of the entrance. If she accepts, she adds a few strands of lining material to the nest and the birds then mate. From then on the male is so busy defending his territory and courting other females that his mate is left to incubate the eggs and feed the young alone.

By contrast, many of the forest wrens of Central America live in faithful pairs all year round. Many are exceptional singers and some, among

▶Once the male Common wren's singing **(1)** has attracted a female, he often starts his courtship display by swooping towards her **(2)**. The result is usually a brief chase **(3)** and often a hurried and unsuccessful attempt to mate **(4)**.

▲The Cactus wren nests among the spines of desert cacti. It finds much of its insect food beneath loose stones.

▶The adaptable Common wren will live almost anywhere except for the centers of large cities and open grassland.

them the delightful Musician wren, engage in beautiful duets.

The much bigger Cactus wren has another breeding system. The birds live in family groups. The parents produce up to four broods in a year, and are helped with feeding duties and territorial defense by the young birds from earlier broods.

THE SHY AND THE BOLD

Despite their loud songs, most wrens are shy, secretive birds that spend most of their time fluttering and scrambling about in low forest undergrowth in search of their insect food. Their small size and dull coloring make them hard to see in their shadowy habitats.

The main exceptions are the Cactus wren and its relatives. These birds are large, with a brighter spotted plumage, and they are much bolder. They live in open scrub and semi-desert habitats, and move about in small family flocks. Staying in groups probably gives them some protection against predators.

THRUSHES

Winter is a difficult time for the resident birds of European gardens. The ground is hard, and there are few insects about. There are snails under the leaves of some of the plants, but how can a bird deal with their tough shells? The Song thrush has found an answer. Grasping a snail by the edge of the shell opening, the bird strikes it against a stone until the shell breaks. It feeds on snails in the summer too.

The thrushes form part of a huge bird family, the Muscicapidae, which comprises 1,394 species spread all over the world. The family includes the true thrushes, described in this article, and also the babblers, warblers and flycatchers (see pages 72-81).

THE ALL-PURPOSE THRUSH

The true thrushes are the real all-rounders of the family. There are about 60 different species and they include the familiar Song thrush and blackbird of Europe, both of which are woodland birds that have adapted easily to life in farmland and city gardens.

Nearly every country except Australia has its own local garden thrush. In South Africa it is the Olive thrush, and in Mexico it is the Clay-colored thrush. In Brazil the Rufous-bellied thrush is the garden inhabitant. However, in North America the position is held by the American robin – a confusing choice of name that goes back to the early European settlers. They took one look at the bird's bright red breast and named it after the popular bird of their homeland.

Many of the true thrushes are renowned for their beautiful songs. These are usually made up of short musical phrases repeated many times over. Some of the birds are also very good mimics, and many a gardener has spent a pleasant half hour or more whistling a duet with the local resident blackbird!

IN PAIRS OR COLONIES

In species that remain in the same habitat all year round, the adult birds usually stay together in faithful pairs.

▼A Song thrush will often take over a particular stone as an "anvil" on which to break snail shells. The ground around it becomes littered with broken shells.

◄The Blue rock thrush inhabits barren rocky areas from Portugal across Europe and Asia to China. In southern Europe it is a common bird of towns and villages.

become quite sociable. They feed together in flocks, and will even roost together at night in cold weather. Most of the northerly species migrate to warmer regions for the winter. The fieldfare, for example, is a winter visitor to Britain and France from its main home in Scandinavia. The tropical members of the family have no winter problems of cold weather or food shortages and so they have no need to migrate.

WHAT TO EAT?

The thrushes of the temperate zone feed mainly on earthworms, slugs and snails, and insects. However, during the winter months, when animal food is scarce, most northern species also feed on berries and on fallen fruit in orchards. Many, such as the blackbird, have become well adapted to town life, and these birds make a good living from the food scraps discarded by people.

The only thrush to take larger prey is the Rock thrush. It lives in rocky mountain habitats from southern Europe across Asia to China, and as well as feeding on insects, this nimble hunter also preys on frogs and small lizards.

GROUND THRUSHES

The ground thrushes are closely related to the true thrushes and are similar in size and shape except for their slightly longer, heavier bills and the striking pattern – often in black and white – on the underside of their wings. They are shy ground-dwelling forest birds found mainly in eastern Asia and Africa.

The only species found outside these regions are White's thrush, which also inhabits Australia, the Varied thrush of the western USA, and the Aztec thrush of Mexico.

They are called "monogamous" pairs, from the Greek words *mono*, one, *gamos*, marriage. During the breeding season the birds defend their nesting territories fiercely against intruders. Their nests are well-built cups of grass and leaves, strengthened with a layer of mud and warmly lined with fine strands of grass. The Song thrush is unusual in that it lines its nest with animal dung or with mud. The female bird shapes and smooths this strange building material by pressing her breast against it and turning round in the nest.

The odd-one-out among the true thrushes is the fieldfare. Instead of holding small individual territories,

fieldfares nest close together in loose colonies. They may take over several adjacent trees, with up to five nests in a single tree. The group behavior also shows in the way the birds defend their nests. If a predator comes near the nest – a cat, a hawk or even an unwary human – the birds will attack by dive-bombing the intruder and spattering it with their droppings. There are even reports of hawks being so heavily plastered with the birds' droppings that they have no longer been able to fly and as a result have eventually starved to death.

During the non-breeding season, most of the all-year resident birds cease their territorial behavior and

The thrush sub-family also includes several other related groups. The robins and the robin-chats are small thrushes of woodlands and tropical forests. They are busy, agile birds that feed mainly on the ground on small insects. One group, the alethes of Africa, have evolved a neat hunting method. They follow closely behind a moving column of army ants and pounce on the insects that they flush out of the undergrowth as the ants march on relentlessly.

Allies of the alethes are the familiar robin of Europe, and also the night-ingale, whose song is one of the most beautiful of all. The nightingale is unusual because it regularly sings at night, both in its summer home in Europe and in its winter home in the savannah regions of Africa.

Unlike most thrushes, the chats and wheatears of Africa and Asia prefer wide open spaces. They inhabit a great variety of open habitats from lightly wooded grasslands to the most barren desert areas. Many of them nest in simple hollows or scrapes in the ground. However, the Desert wheat-ear, which lives in the semi-desert scrublands of central Asia, will often make its nest up to 4ft deep in an abandoned rodent burrow. Nesting underground in this way protects the bird from the heat of the day and from the bitter cold of the desert night. One race of this species even nests at 11,500ft on the bleak Tibetan plateau.

▲The robin is one of the most familiar and popular birds in Britain, but over much of Europe it is a shy woodland species. The bird defends territories in both summer and winter, and the male uses its bright red breast in its threat displays to chase away rival males.

▶A Western bluebird at its nest hole in the forests of California in May. This species is found throughout western North America, from Canada in the north to Mexico in the south.

BABBLERS

At dawn and dusk the forests of Burma are alive with bird calls, but none is stranger than the chorus of the White-crested laughing thrush. With their crests raised, several of these birds dance together on the forest floor, their raucous laughter-like calls ringing louder and louder. As one group's chorus dies away it is replaced by the cries of nearby groups until the forested hills echo with the sounds of calling birds.

The laughing thrushes are about the size of crows, and are the biggest members of the babbler sub-family. At the other end of the size range are tiny birds the size of wrens and tits. In between are a host of small- and medium-sized birds living in habitats as varied as forests and mountains, scrubland and semi-deserts. Babblers are birds from the Old World and they are spread across Africa and the Middle East to India and the islands of South-east Asia. Only one species is found in the Americas, and that is the tiny Wren-tit that inhabits the coast of Oregon and California.

The babblers are an ancient sub-family which has its "headquarters" in the forests of tropical Asia, especially in the many isolated mountain chains of that region. The babblers have evolved in many scattered separate groups, and as a result they include species that at first glance look (and behave) like tits, or wrens, or jays or shrikes. This is why so many of them have been given combination names like tit-babbler and wren-babbler.

GLEANERS AND DIGGERS
The various different babblers have specialized in many different life-styles. Many of the smaller species glean their insect food from the leaves of the forest canopy or from cracks in

BABBLERS Timaliinae
(*252 species*)

Habitat: varied, from mountain and desert to tropical forest.

Diet: mainly insects.

Breeding: 2-6 eggs incubated for 14-15 days in an open or domed nest usually in a bush or tree.

Size: length 4-14in; weight 1/5-5 ounces.

Plumage: many species have camouflage patterns of brown and gray; tropical forest species often have splashes of bright color.

Species mentioned in text:
Arabian babbler (*Turdoides squamiceps*)
Black-capped sibia (*Heterophasia capistrata*)
Common babbler (*Turdoides caudatus*)
Jungle babbler (*T. striatus*)
Rusty-cheeked scimitar babbler (*Pomatorhinus erythrogenys*)
White-crested laughing thrush (*Garrulax leucolophus*)
Wren-tit (*Chamaea fasciata*)

▲ **Two of the world's babblers** The White-crested laughing thrush (1) of the forests of the Himalayas, Thailand, Burma and Sumatra, with its white crest raised and producing its call. The Pied babbler (*Turdoides bicolor*) (2) of southern Africa in typical position.

tree bark. The larger species are more likely to search for their food on the forest floor, digging among the leaf litter and turning over bits of dead wood to get at the adult insects and grubs beneath. One of the most highly specialized of all is the Black-capped sibia of the Himalayas, which drinks the sweet sap oozing from holes in tree bark. Although it is not related to the woodpecker family, this bird has almost the same life-style as the North American sapsucker (see page 44).

LIVING IN PARTIES
The Common babbler and the Jungle babbler are among the most widespread birds in India. They are as common in gardens and on roadside

►The Arabian babbler inhabits thinly vegetated wadis (dry stream-beds) in the harsh open desert regions of North Africa, the Middle East and Iran.

verges as they are in their natural woodland habitats, and are often seen roving through the trees in noisy groups of up to 15 birds. These so-called parties are usually extended families – that is, they are made up of closely related birds. The whole party helps to incubate the eggs laid by the senior female and to gather food for the nestlings once the clutch has hatched. Each party of Jungle babblers claims a territory and defends it against neighbouring ones. Border squabbles are frequent and noisy, and the birds often end up fighting.

The related laughing thrushes have a similar way of life, but they often spend the day in parties of up to 100 birds. In the evening the parties split up and the birds roost for the night in groups of up to 10, gathering together again first thing in the morning.

◄Scimitar babblers like the Rusty-cheeked species of southern Asia and China search for food among dense leafy vegetation close to the ground.

73

OLD WORLD WARBLERS

In the fading light of a fall evening, a tiny Willow warbler leaves its summer home in Siberia on the first leg of an annual journey that will take it 7,200 miles away to the wooded savannahs south of the Sahara Desert. For 3 weeks the bird has been feeding almost constantly, doubling its body-weight with reserves of fat to provide the fuel for this incredible journey.

▼ **Three of Europe's summer visitors** The blackcap (*Sylvia atricapilla*) **(1)** is a year-round resident of Spain, France and Italy, but birds from farther north winter in Africa. The Sedge warbler **(2)** and the Reed warbler **(3)** spend the summer in Europe and winter in Africa.

The annual migrations of small European and Asian songbirds are one of the wonders of the bird world. Somehow it seems natural that birds such as storks, eagles and albatrosses should make long journeys; their enormous wings are just made for such feats. But most of the woodland warblers would fit easily into the palm of a person's hand. Some are only half the size of a sparrow.

HAZARDOUS JOURNEYS

It seems almost impossible that creatures so small should be capable of flying such vast distances, even without the added dangers of storms and headwinds, "sportsmen" with shotguns, and the hawks and falcons that lie in wait to ambush them.

Long sections of these journeys must be made across barren lands, so

OLD WORLD WARBLERS Sylviinae
(339 species)

● ◨ ☠

◼ **Habitat:** dense vegetation.

◩ **Diet:** mainly insects; some fruit.

○ **Breeding:** 2-7 pale-colored eggs incubated for 12-14 days.

Size: length 3½-6in; weight ⅙-⅔ ounce.

Plumage: mainly dull brown, green or yellow, often with darker streaks.

Species mentioned in text:
Dartford warbler (*Sylvia undata*)
Great reed warbler (*Acrocephalus arundinaceus*)
Marsh warbler (*Acrocephalus palustris*)
Red-faced crombec (*Sylvietta whytii*)
Reed warbler (*Acrocephalus scirpaceus*)
Sedge warbler (*A. schoenobaenus*)
Spectacled warbler (*Sylvia conspicillata*)
Subalpine warbler (*S. cantillans*)
Whitethroat (*S. communis*)
Willow warblers (genus *Phylloscopus*)

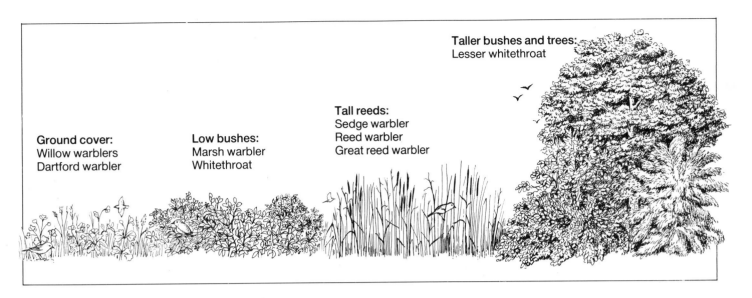

Taller bushes and trees:
Lesser whitethroat

Tall reeds:
Sedge warbler
Reed warbler
Great reed warbler

Ground cover:
Willow warblers
Dartford warbler

Low bushes:
Marsh warbler
Whitethroat

the birds must carry their "fuel" with them. Most warblers feed up on insects until they are at least one-third heavier than normal. The Sedge warbler, like the Willow warbler, takes this to the extreme. From a normal body-weight of just ⅓ ounce, it may "take on fuel" until it weighs ⅔ ounce. The extra fat is stored all over the body, even under the eyelids, and the bird may end up like a feather-covered ball, barely able to take off. But none of this is "excess baggage". Even after a good flight most of the birds arrive in their winter quarters exhausted and in need of food and water.

The return journey in the spring is no easier. The birds are flying into the wind for most of the way. And even after a final bout of feeding in the marshes around Lake Chad, they must stop again to recover their strength as soon as they have crossed the Sahara Desert and reached the safety of North Africa.

LIMITED SUPPLIES OF FOOD
The reason why so many warblers migrate in winter is that these birds feed entirely on insects. In the cold months of winter there is simply not enough food around for the birds of the northern regions, so most of them head for warmer parts. The few that

do remain in Europe in winter are often badly hit by food shortages. About 80 years ago, the Dartford warbler was found in dry heathlands across most of southern Britain. Since then a great deal of its habitat has been destroyed. In 1961 there were fewer than 500 pairs left, and this small population was almost wiped out by the severe winters of the early 1960s. By 1963 there were only 11 pairs remaining. The total has slowly re-covered to about 400 pairs again, but this attractive bird is still one of Britain's rarest and most endangered species.

FEEDING STRATEGIES
Typical warblers are small and dull-colored birds with narrow, finely pointed bills and strong feet that are thoroughly adapted for scrambling and perching. They live in many different habitats, from grasslands to marshes and forests, but always in dense vegetation, where they scurry about in search of insects.

At first it seems as if all the warblers in a particular habitat must be com-peting for the same food, but the birds have evolved strategies to avoid this. Many species claim feeding territories and defend them not just against their own species, but also against any

▲ Within a temperate grassland and woodland area such as this there may be many different species of warbler. Each will nest in and occupy a particular type of vegetation. This ensures that safe nest sites are shared out and that all the birds can feed without wasting energy on unnecessary fighting and chasing.

▲ The Red-faced crombec inhabits dry savannah and scrubland from Sudan south to Mozambique. The birds often feed in pairs or in small family groups, along with other species of warbler.

other bird that tries to move in and forage there. In other cases, warblers feed quite peacefully in the same area by sharing the food between them. Large warblers, for example, may concentrate on the bigger insects and leave the smaller ones to their smaller relatives.

The Reed warbler and the Great reed warbler usually take similar food, but if both species are nesting in the same reed-bed they choose different diets for their nestlings and so avoid fighting over the food available.

The crombecs of East Africa have found a different solution. Where a few species occur in the same area, one or two of them will feed low in the vegetation, while the others (such as the Red-faced crombec) feed higher up.

▲The Spectacled warbler is a short-range migrant, spending the summer in Europe and the winter in North Africa.

SINGERS AND SONGS

The fact that these birds have been given the name "warblers" gives some idea how important songs and calls are in their lives.

Most of the birds live in dense vegetation where visibility is blocked by the foliage, so they use their voices to attract their mates, and to warn intruders that they are trespassing on someone else's territory.

Although some of the larger species have quite harsh voices, many of the smaller ones are very musical. It is often the best singers, like the Sedge warbler and the Reed warbler, that are the first to find mates.

Some species are rather good mimics, but the Marsh warbler must surely be the best. Its song is made up entirely of the songs of other birds! The warbler may use 80 or more "borrowed" songs, half of them belonging to African birds that it has heard in its winter quarters.

◀The Subalpine warbler inhabits sunny hillsides up to 6,600ft above sea level. It breeds in southern Europe, nesting low down in gorse and bramble bushes.

▲A whitethroat darts into a woodland thicket. In its mating display, the male bird flies high into the sky, singing loudly, then tumbles earthward again.

SCATTERED RELATIVES

The warblers are mainly birds of the Old World – of Africa, Europe and Asia. Out of 339 species, 15 occur in North America, Australia has 8, and New Zealand just 1.

The scattered islands of the Indian Ocean and Pacific Ocean are home to some of the world's rarest warblers. Many are threatened because the dense thickets in which they live have been cut down to make way for agriculture. But one native Hawaiian species of warbler became extinct about 70 years ago because the vegetation of its island home was destroyed by introduced rabbits. Today the rarest species is a warbler of Aldabra Island in the Indian Ocean. It has not been seen for over 5 years.

▶This gnatcatcher, photographed in South America, is one of the few species of Old World warbler that is found in the Americas.

WOOD WARBLERS

In a spruce forest in eastern North America, a scientist is studying a group of brightly colored birds feeding among the leaves and branches of a single tree. He can see at least five different species, and each is using a different part of the tree. It is a perfect example of ecological sharing and specialization.

Wood warblers are highly organized birds. They are the most varied and abundant forest-dwelling birds in North America. They are most common in the eastern half and in some areas there they can account for as much as 70 per cent of the birdlife found in spruce forests.

In such forests, wood warblers of the large genus *Dendroica* are the most widespread. One species gleans insects from the tips of the topmost branches. Another scurries about and forages for food on the trunk. A third feeds among dense foliage, while a fourth searches among the leaves of the outer canopy. The fifth species prefers a little more space and is feeding on the ground beneath the tree. In this habitat, in summer, food is plentiful. There is simply no need for the birds to compete, and by specializing in this way they can feed close to each other without squabbling and fighting.

Most of the wood warblers have narrow, finely pointed bills that are ideal for gleaning insects from the tiny crevices in tree bark and from among the leaves. A few, however, catch their insect food on the wing, and they have broad bills, rather like those of tyrant flycatchers (see page 50). Others, like the water-thrushes, feed mostly on the ground and have longer, stronger bills than their tree-feeding relatives. One species has adopted the life-style of a nuthatch, scurrying about the trunks and branches of large trees.

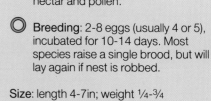

WOOD WARBLERS
Parulidae (*120 species*)

⬤ ◧ ☠

◺ Habitat: forest and brushland.

◨ Diet: mainly insects; some fruit, nectar and pollen.

◯ Breeding: 2-8 eggs (usually 4 or 5), incubated for 10-14 days. Most species raise a single brood, but will lay again if nest is robbed.

Size: length 4-7in; weight ¼-¾ ounce.

Plumage: brightly colored in most species. Females not as bright as males.

Species mentioned in text:
American redstart (*Setophaga ruticilla*)
Yellow warbler (*Dendroica petechia*)
Yellow-rumped warbler (*D. coronata*)

COLORFUL TRAVELERS
The wood warblers are among the most colorful of America's birds. Many of the tree-dwelling species are bright blue, yellow, red or orange, decorated on the wings and tail with brilliant white bars. Ground-dwelling species are more at risk from predators so they tend to be less colorful. Most are brown or olive green and some have white-speckled breasts, which is why several species are called thrushes.

Like many insect-eaters, most wood warblers are migrants. Birds from the northern regions head south to Mexico, Central America and the northern part of South America for the winter. Some also change their feeding habits outside the breeding season and feed partly on fruit, nectar and pollen. The Yellow-rumped warbler feeds mainly on bayberry and wax myrtle in winter.

FAMILY LIFE
Many of these wood warblers have an elaborate courtship behavior, with intricate display flights and special courtship songs.

Once they have paired, the birds build well-made nests of woven grass, either on the ground or in a tree. In most species it is the female that

▲A female American redstart on the nest, which has been made not only with twigs and grass, but, unusually, with paper and wood shavings.

▶A female Yellow warbler presents her brood with a beakful of juicy caterpillars.

incubates the eggs and feeds the newly hatched young. As the chicks get bigger, the male bird helps to feed them. Once the young have left the nest it is common for some of them to go off into the forest with the father and some with the mother.

The parents continue to feed the young for up to 2 weeks after they leave the nest.

OLD WORLD FLYCATCHERS

Leaving his mate on her nest in an old woodpecker hole, a male Pied flycatcher flits away through a European woodland. Anyone seeing him leave might think he was simply going off to feed. But this flying Romeo has other plans. A few hundred yards away, safely out of sight, he has set up another territory – and there he is busily courting a second female!

▼All over the world there are red-breasted birds that European settlers have named "robins." This Australian flycatcher is called a Red-capped robin.

OLD WORLD FLY-CATCHERS Sub-family Muscicapinae (*156 species*)

Habitat: woodland, forest and scrub, from sea level to 13,000ft.

  Diet: mainly insects, some fruit.

Breeding: 1-8 eggs (usually 2-6), incubated for 12-14 days.

Size: length 4-8in; weights not known.

Plumage: some species plain gray or brown, others brightly colored.

Species mentioned in text:
Blue-and-white flycatcher (*Ficedula cyanomelana*)
Pied flycatcher (*F. hypoleuca*)
Red-capped robin (*Petroica goodenovii*)
Spotted flycatcher (*Muscicapa striata*)
White-eyed slaty flycatcher (*Dioptrornis fischeri*)

The extraordinary behavior of the male Pied flycatcher is yet another of nature's ways of making sure that the breeding male produces as many young as possible.

WOODLAND CHEAT

When the male arrives in Europe in spring from tropical Africa, he claims a territory round a suitable nest-hole and sets about attracting a mate and breeding with her. If he succeeds, he rushes off and tries again in another territory, behaving exactly like a bachelor male as he courts every new female he sees. If he is lucky once more, he will breed with a second female and she too will lay eggs. The male then leaves her to bring up her family alone, and goes back to help his "number one" mate raise her brood.

But the story is not quite that simple. While the male is away from home looking for a second mate, one of his neighbors will often sneak in and breed with his first partner. At the end of the season he may really be the father of only about three-quarters of the chicks raised in his nest. But the two-mate male is still better off than one that remains faithful to a single female. This is because he too has to leave the nest at times to chase rival males from his territory, and in those brief absences another male will often rush in and breed with his partner.

The male Pied flycatcher has clearly evolved the strategy: if you cannot be sure of being the father of all the young in your nest, having two mates increases the total number of young that are definitely yours.

LEGS, BILLS AND FEEDING

The Old World flycatchers are found throughout most of Europe, Africa, Asia, Australia and the islands of the Pacific. They are small birds of woodland habitats, and many of them hunt by dashing from a perch to catch their insect prey in flight – hence the name flycatcher. A Spotted flycatcher may dash out to snatch a passing insect about three times a minute.

Most of the species that hunt in this way have broad, flat bills with bristles around the nostrils. Their legs and feet are quite weak as they spend most of their time sitting still. In comparison, many Australian species take most of their food on the ground. They have finer, pointed bills and stronger legs.

Although insects form their main diet, many flycatchers also take other foods as well. The Blue-and-white flycatcher of Borneo feeds on many different fruits and berries, and the White-eyed slaty flycatcher of Africa is even known to prey on the nestlings of other birds.

Most European and Asian species, like the Pied flycatcher, migrate to Africa, India or South-east Asia for the winter. Tropical species remain in the same habitat all year, though mountain-dwelling species will often move down to lower levels outside the breeding season.

▼**Two of the Old World flycatchers** The Flame robin (*Petroica phoenicea*) **(1)** of South-east Australia and Tasmania and the Pied flycatcher **(2)** of Europe, Asia and Africa. Pied flycatchers from as far north as Siberia pass through Spain on their way to winter quarters in Africa.

TITS AND CHICKADEES

It is April in a woodland in Central Europe. A female Great tit has started to lay her eggs. Each egg will weigh about one-tenth of her own body-weight, and she may lay as many as 10 eggs. Over a laying period of just 10 to 14 days, this small woodland and garden bird will have produced her own weight in eggs.

To perform this remarkable biological feat, the female Great tit requires an enormous amount of food. Not only has she to form the eggs inside her body, but she must also keep up her own strength and fitness. The male Great tit helps by bringing food to the female all the time she is laying, and the female times her egg-laying to coincide with a good supply of food.

SHARED PARENT CARE
Tits are popular garden birds, and people often put out food for them early in the spring when their natural food is still scarce. This is why garden-living tits often lay much earlier than wild tits in the same area.

The eggs hatch after about 14 days, but the female usually continues to brood the chicks for another 4 to 5

TITS AND CHICKADEES Paridae (*46 species*), Aegithalidae (*7*), Remizidae (*9*)

long-tailed and penduline tits 6-10. Incubated for 13-14 days.

Size: length 3½-6in, weight ⅙-⅔ ounce, except Sultan tit, which reaches 9in and weighs 1 ounce.

Plumage: mainly brown, white, gray and black; three species with bright blue.

Species mentioned in text:
Blue tit (*Parus caeruleus*)
Bushtit (*Psaltriparus minimus*)
Cape penduline tit (*Anthoscopus minutus*)
Great tit (*Parus major*)
Penduline tit (*Remiz pendulinus*)
Long-tailed tit (*Aegithalos caudatus*)
Sultan tit (*Melanochlora sultanea*)
Willow tit (*Parus montanus*)

● ■

◢ Habitat: woodland and scrub.

◢ Diet: mainly insects, some seeds.

◯ Breeding: true tits 4-12 eggs;

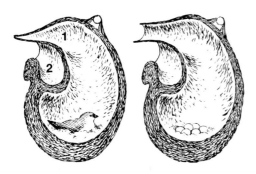

▲ The Cape penduline tit builds a false entrance into its nest, probably to keep out predators. The real entrance (1) is above the false one (2). The nest's springy construction keeps the real entrance closed (left) most of the time, but the tit can open it easily (right).

days to keep them warm. After that, feeding the nestlings is a full-time job for both parents. Caterpillars are the main food, and with a large brood of hungry nestlings each parent may have to make 500 journeys a day carrying beakfuls of food to the nest. Most tits produce one brood a year, but the tireless Great tit will often raise a second brood if food is plentiful.

COLORFUL AND SOCIABLE
These small, busy, woodland and scrub dwellers are divided into three families. True tits – the Paridae – (called titmice and chickadees in the USA) are the most widespread, and with 46 species also the most numerous. They are found everywhere except Australia, Madagascar and South America, in wooded habitats from sea level to mountaintops. They are all similar in general appearance and are among the easiest of birds to recognize. They have short sturdy bills, short legs, and are superb acrobats, often hanging upside down on twigs to feed. Many are brown, or gray and white, but a few, including the Blue tit, have yellow and blue plumage.

Most of the true tits establish territories in winter or early in spring, and defend them against all comers. The territories are usually abandoned at the end of the breeding season, but some species keep their territories all year. In Scandinavia the Willow tit often winters in small groups that share a territory.

The seven species of long-tailed tits (family Aegithalidae) are tiny, sociable birds that live in flocks of 6 to 12 birds for much of the year. They build the most beautiful nests of feathers and moss, bound together with spiders' webs and camouflaged with a covering of lichen. Among the Long-tailed tit of Europe and the bushtit of North America birds with young in the nest are often helped by others whose own eggs have been taken by predators or otherwise failed.

The third family, the penduline tits (Remizidae), are found in Africa, Europe and Asia, and in North and Central America. They are named after their hanging purse-like nests of woven grass, moss and feathers.

Penduline tits spend most of the year in small parties, and the main

habitat for most members of the family is open scrub woodland. The one exception is the Penduline tit itself, which prefers dense scrub and reed marshes along rivers and lakes. This species often nests in small willow and tamarisk trees and feeds on insects and seeds from among the riverside vegetation.

▲ **Typical members of the tit group**
A group of Long-tailed tits (1) roosting close together for warmth. A Chinese yellow tit (*Parus spilonotus*) (2). Blue tit (3) in flight and with a garden nestbox. A verdin (*Auriparus flavifrons*) (4), one of the penduline tit family. An Azure tit (*Parus cyanus*) (5), and a close-up of the Bridled titmouse (*P. wollweberi*) (6) with caterpillar.

NUTHATCHES

In 1975 an exciting discovery was made high in the mountains of Algeria. On the ridge of Djebel Babor, thickly wooded with cedars, oaks and Algerian firs, scientists found a small population of tiny gray and white birds. They were quickly identified as nuthatches. This was a new species, never seen before, and its survival was already threatened by the destruction of the forest.

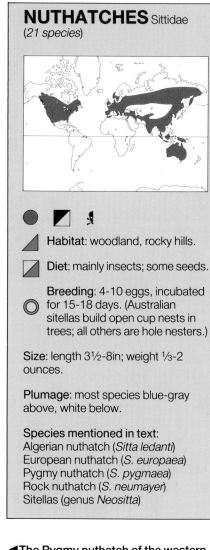

NUTHATCHES Sittidae
(*21 species*)

● ◨ 🐾

◹ **Habitat:** woodland, rocky hills.

◹ **Diet:** mainly insects; some seeds.

○ **Breeding:** 4-10 eggs, incubated for 15-18 days. (Australian sitellas build open cup nests in trees; all others are hole nesters.)

Size: length 3½-8in; weight ⅓-2 ounces.

Plumage: most species blue-gray above, white below.

Species mentioned in text:
Algerian nuthatch (*Sitta ledanti*)
European nuthatch (*S. europaea*)
Pygmy nuthatch (*S. pygmaea*)
Rock nuthatch (*S. neumayer*)
Sitellas (genus *Neositta*)

◀The Pygmy nuthatch of the western USA is the smallest member of the family.

The discovery of the Algerian nuthatch came just in the nick of time. In a few more years the only exclusively North African member of the nuthatch family would have disappeared forever. In this case the threat did not come from deliberate cutting of the forest, but from grazing goats and cattle.

In summer, herdsmen take their animals into the high mountains to find refuge from the heat. The problem for the nuthatch was that the grazing animals were preventing any new young trees from growing, and the forest was slowly shrinking as old trees died.

Luckily, the Algerian nuthatch became the focus of a conservation campaign, and as long as the forest remains protected the future of this rare African species should be safe.

TREE-TRUNK ACROBATICS

The nuthatches are quite unique in the bird world for they are the only woodland birds that can run as fast head-first down tree trunks as they can run up them! Woodpeckers and treecreepers cling to a tree trunk with their feet at roughly the same level, and use their strong stiff tail feathers for extra support. A nuthatch has no need for an extra prop. It always places one foot higher on the tree than the other, so that it hangs from the upper foot while supporting itself with the lower one. In this way it can move up, down or round the tree with equal ease.

The 21 species of true nuthatch are found in woodland and parkland habitats across North America, and from western Europe east to China and South-east Asia.

◀▼ **Typical nuthatch postures and poses** A Corsican nuthatch (*Sitta white-headii*) **(1)** feeding – with one foot, as always, higher than the other. The same species uses feeding in its courtship **(2)**. A European nuthatch **(3)** in threat posture and **(4)** in defensive pose.

In Australia and New Guinea there are no true nuthatches, but the family is represented by two closely related birds called sitellas.

The birds are all similar in size, color and behavior. Most are soft blue-gray above and white below, with long, needle-sharp bills for probing for insects and spiders in the tiny crevices and holes in tree bark. The Rock nuthatch of southern Europe and the Middle East differs from most of its relatives by living on rocky hillsides and in dry scrubland. In addition to spiders and insects it also includes small snails in its diet.

Although nuthatches feed mainly on insects, the more northerly ones eat seeds as well. They jam the seeds firmly into cracks in the bark then crack them open with sharp blows of the bill. In fact, the family got its name from the European nuthatch's fondness for hazelnuts. Some of these birds take tree seeds in the fall and store them under clumps of moss or in crevices in tree bark for use later in the winter. European nuthatches have been seen making up to 900 trips in a single day as they prepared a winter store of sunflower seeds.

DIGGERS AND PLASTERERS

All the nuthatches of the genus *Sitta* nest in holes. Some will take over any available tree-hole, while others excavate their own chambers in rotten wood. If the entrance to a hole is too large for safety, some species will make it narrower by plastering the edges with mud until it is only just wide enough for the bird to squeeze through. The Rock nuthatch, for example, lives on dry hillsides. It creates a safe nest by building a curved mud wall across the entrance to a cavity among the rocks. The nest may even have a specially made tube-like entrance for extra safety. If mud is hard to find, this versatile builder uses animal dung, or occasionally even crushed caterpillars.

TREECREEPERS

Pausing every few seconds to pick off an insect or spider, a Common treecreeper makes its way up the trunk of a Redwood tree and out along a branch. It then flies smoothly down to the base of the next tree and starts all over again.

TREECREEPERS
Certhiidae (*6 species*), Climacteridae (*6*), Rhabdornithidae (*2*)

 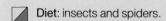

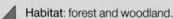 Habitat: forest and woodland.

Diet: insects and spiders.

Breeding: *Certhia* species 3-9 eggs, others 2 or 3. Incubation 14 or 15 days in the Certhiidae, 16-23 days in the Climacteridae.

Size: length 5-7in; weight ¼-1¼ ounces.

Plumage: patterns of brown and black, often with paler undersides.

Species mentioned in text:
Brown treecreeper (*Climacteris picumnus*)
Common treecreeper (*Certhia familiaris*)
Red-browed treecreeper (*Climacteris erythrops*)
Spotted creeper (*Salpornis spilonotus*)
White-throated treecreeper (*Climacteris leucophaea*)

▶ The White-throated treecreeper is a common resident of the eucalyptus forests of south-eastern Australia.

The Common treecreeper's unusual feeding method makes it one of the easiest woodland birds to recognize. As it spirals up a tree trunk, it looks very like a small brown mouse. Often it is only the swooping flight that gives the bird away as its mostly brown plumage provides it with almost perfect camouflage against the rough bark of the forest trees.

The bird climbs with a busy scurrying movement, not hurried, but never still for more than a few seconds. Its toes are equipped with long, curved claws, and its bill too is long and slightly curved to enable the bird to probe behind loose flakes of bark in its search for spiders and grubs.

WOODLAND SPECIALISTS
There are three families of treecreepers. The Holarctic species (Certhiidae) live in North America, Africa and Eurasia. Australasian treecreepers (Climacteridae) are found only in Australia and New Guinea. The two species of Philippine creepers (Rhabdornithidae) inhabit the forests of the Philippine Islands. Little is known about this last group.

The Common treecreeper, known as the Brown creeper in North America, is the most widespread of the six Northern Hemisphere species. It is found in coniferous forests right across North America, and through Europe and Asia from Spain to China and Japan. Like the rest of its family, the Common treecreeper has an extra climbing aid which the Australasian birds do not have. Its tail feathers are long and pointed and have stiff central shafts. The bird uses them as a prop while climbing up trees, in the same way that woodpeckers do.

CONCEALED NESTS

The Common treecreeper's nest is well hidden in a small hole dug in the soft bark of trees, or tucked behind a flap of loose bark or beneath the ivy covering a tree trunk. Breeding pairs first make a platform of strong twigs. They then build the nest on top, weaving it from strips of grass and bark and lining it with feathers and wool. The nest is often oval or sometimes boat-shaped.

Odd-one-out in the northern family is the Spotted creeper. It does not have stiff tail feathers, and its nests are constructed on a horizontal branch, usually in a fork. The breeding pair usually build a neat cup-shaped nest, which they camouflage beautifully with spiders' webs and lichen.

The Australasian treecreepers are slightly bigger and heavier than the other treecreepers and some, like the Brown treecreeper, also spend much of their time on the ground. Their social behavior is also much more varied. Species such as the White-throated treecreeper are solitary for most of the year and only pair up in the breeding season. The Red-browed treecreeper and some other species live in pairs or small groups, and during the breeding season the non-breeding birds help to feed the breeding females and their young.

▼The treecreeper's feeding method is highly efficient. The bird feeds busily while climbing, then glides effortlessly to the next tree. It works its way through a wood like a roller-coaster.

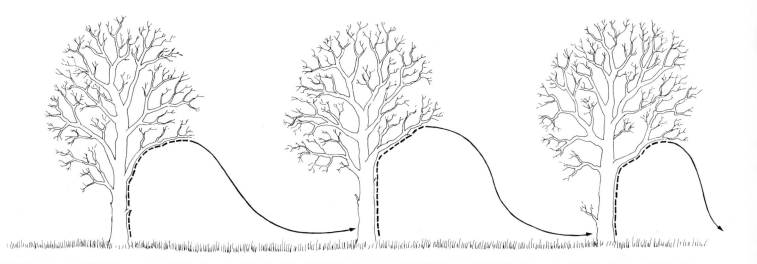

VIREOS

A Yellow-throated vireo feeding high in the canopy of a Californian forest repeats the same short phrase over and over again. Its song is not very musical, but the bird is a most persistent singer. It hardly pauses from singing even when capturing and eating a large insect!

The Yellow-throated vireo, like all vireos, is a small woodland, scrub and forest bird found only in the New World. Vireos resemble some of the wood warblers in appearance, but their bills are much thicker and heavier and in most species the tip of the upper bill has a small hook. The other main difference is in the way the birds feed. While the wood warblers are busy feeders, forever darting here and there among the foliage, the vireos are much more methodical. A feeding bird will move quite slowly and will carefully search for insects all around and under a leaf before moving on to the next one.

WHO FEEDS WHERE?

Most of the vireos eat a certain amount of fruit, both in summer and in winter, but the birds' main diet consists of spiders and winged insects. The Red-eyed and the Yellow-throated vireos usually feed high in the forest canopy, taking their prey from the leaves and twigs. Occasionally they will feed in flight and snatch a passing insect. The White-eyed vireo and most of the other scrub-dwelling species feed much lower down in the trees, but only one species – the Gray vireo – ever feeds on the ground. Unlike most of its family, this species is found in the canyons and scrub

▼The Red-eyed vireo is one of the most common birds in the deciduous forests of the eastern USA. It is also one of the most persistent singers.

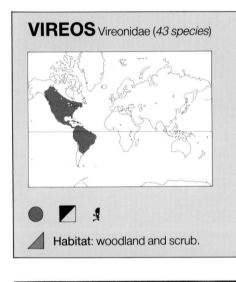

VIREOS Vireonidae (*43 species*)

◨ Diet: insects, spiders, fruit.

◯ Breeding: usually 2 eggs in tropical species; 4 or 5 in temperate species; incubated for 11-13 days.

Size: length 4-6in; weight ⅓-⅔ ounce.

Plumage: mainly green above, yellow or white below. Some species brown above.

Species mentioned in text:
Gray vireo (*Vireo vicinior*)
Hutton's vireo (*V. huttoni*)
Red-eyed vireo (*V. olivaceus*)
White-eyed vireo (*V. griseus*)
Yellow-throated vireo (*V. flavifrons*)

● ◨ ☡

◣ Habitat: woodland and scrub.

vegetation of semi-desert areas where food is scarce, so it must feed wherever it can.

COPING WITH WINTER

For vireos of the tropical zone winter presents no problem. Food is plentiful all year round, and these species do not migrate. Many of the birds seem to maintain territories throughout the year, and during the winter months they live in pairs or in small family groups.

For the temperate-zone species, winter is a more serious matter. Some residents form flocks containing unrelated species that roam the countryside in search of food. Hutton's vireo, for example, often joins flocks of chickadees and nuthatches. The Red-eyed vireo, on the other hand, may travel 3,000 miles from its summer quarters in Canada and the USA to wintering grounds in Cuba and in central South America.

NESTS AND NEST INVADERS

A typical vireo nest is a coarsely woven bag of leaves and bark strips bound together with spiders' webs and decorated on the outside with spiders' egg cases and bits of moss. The nest can take from 4 to 25 days to build, depending on the species, and in most cases male and female birds share the task.

The eggs are laid as soon as the nest is finished. The female does most of the incubating, but in many species the male also helps. He looks after the eggs while his mate temporarily leaves the nest to feed.

One of the biggest dangers that faces vireos in the temperate-zone comes from the Brown-headed cowbird, which lays its eggs in the vireos' nests. This reduces the number of vireo chicks raised. However, some species do fight back. A few toss the cowbird's eggs out of their nests, while others pile on extra nest material until the cowbird's eggs are completely buried.

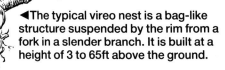

◀The typical vireo nest is a bag-like structure suspended by the rim from a fork in a slender branch. It is built at a height of 3 to 65ft above the ground.

▼Pepper-shrikes, such as this species, and shrike-vireos, are closely related to vireos, but differ in having brightly colored facial markings.

GLOSSARY

Aerial Associated with the air. Birds such as swifts, which take all their food on the wing, are called "aerial hunters."

Aggression Any behavior in which one animal attacks or threatens another.

Air sacs Little air-filled bags in a bird's body connected to its lungs that help increase the amount of air the bird breathes in.

Aquatic Living in or near the water. *See also* Marine.

Bill Also called beak; the horny part of a bird's mouth with which it gathers food.

Brood The group of young raised in a single breeding cycle.

Call The sounds a bird makes.

Camouflage Color and patterns on an animal's coat that allow it to blend in with its surroundings.

Carnivore An animal that feeds mainly on the flesh of other animals.

Carrion Meat from a dead animal.

Class The division of animal classification above Order.

Clutch The eggs a bird lays in one breeding session.

Colony A large group of birds of the same species gathered together for the breeding season.

Competition The contest between two or more species over such things as space and food.

Conservation Preserving and protecting living things, their habitat and the environment in general.

Courtship The period when an animal tries to attract a mate, or renews its bonds with a mate from previous years.

Crustaceans Small marine and freshwater animals with hard outer shells. The group includes the crabs, shrimps, krill, copepods and lobsters.

Display A typical pattern of behavior associated with important aspects of an animal's life, such as courtship, mating, nesting and defending territory.

Diurnal Active during the day.

Endangered species One whose numbers have dropped so low that it is in danger of becoming extinct.

Environment The surroundings, of a particular species, or the world about us in general.

Extinction The complete loss of a species, either locally or on the Earth.

Eyrie The nest of a bird of prey such as an eagle, usually sited high on a cliff.

Family The division of animal classification below Order and above Genus. In the bird world there are 163 recognized families.

Fledging The time when a young bird first takes to the air; a fledgling is a bird that has just begun to fly.

Flight feathers The large feathers on the wings, which are divided into the primaries and secondaries.

Flock A large group of birds whose members habitually move around together.

Foraging Going in search of food.

Gape The extent to which a bird's bill can open.

Genus The division of animal classification below Family and above Species. In the bird world there are 1,975 recognized genera.

Gizzard The muscular forepart of a bird's stomach in which hard food is ground; well developed in seed-eating birds such as finches.

Habitat The type of surroundings in which an animal lives.

Hatching The moment when a young bird emerges from the egg; hence *hatchling*, a young bird that has recently hatched.

Home range The area in which an animal usually lives and feeds.

Incubation The period during which a bird sits on a clutch of eggs to keep them warm so that they will develop and eventually hatch.

Insectivores Animals that live chiefly on insects.

Invertebrates Animals without backbones, such as insects and worms.

Larva The grub or caterpillar of an insect. The plural is *larvae*.

Lek An area of ground where some birds display.

Mammals Animals whose females have mammary glands, which produce milk on which they feed their young.

Mandibles The two parts that make up a bird's bill.

Marine Associated with the sea, or living in the sea.

Migration The long-distance movement of animals. It is typically seasonal, e.g. between far northern breeding grounds in summer and warmer southern regions in winter.

Molluscs Soft-bodied animals, usually with protective shells, including land snails, cockles, mussels and limpets.

Molt The period during which a bird sheds old feathers and grows new ones.

Monogamous Having only one mate. Some birds stay paired for life. Others just for a breeding season.

Nestling A young bird in the nest.

Nocturnal Active during the night.

Nomadic Wandering; having no fixed home territory. Waxwings appear to be nomads, nesting each year where the food is most plentiful.

Omnivore An animal that has a varied diet, eating both plants and animals.

Order The division of animal classification below Class and above Family. There are 28 recognized orders in the bird world.

Passerines Perching birds – those belonging to the order Passeriformes, for example wrens, tits and finches.

Plumage The feathers of a bird. Many birds have a different plumage in the spring and summer breeding season from that in the winter. The breeding plumage is often vivid, the winter plumage dull.

Polygamous An animal that has more than one mate; most often this applies to males.

Population A separate group of animals of the same species.

Predator An animal that hunts and kills other animals, its prey.

Preening Running the bill through the feathers to keep the plumage clean and airworthy. The action also distributes oil onto the plumage from a preen gland just above the tail.

Prey The animals that are hunted by a predator. The word is also a verb, so an eagle is said to prey on rabbits.

Primaries The long outer flight feathers on the wings, with which a bird propels itself through the air.

Race The division of animal classification below Sub-species; it refers to animals that are very similar but have slightly different characteristics.

Raptor Another name for a bird of prey such as eagles and hawks. Vultures are not considered raptors.

Regurgitate Bring up food previously swallowed.

Resident An animal that stays in the same area all year round.

Rodents Small animals of the rat, mouse and squirrel order. They are prey for many hunting birds.

Roosting Sleeping or resting.

Savannah Tropical grassland, particularly in Africa.

Scrape A hollow in the ground made by an animal in which it lays its eggs.

Secondaries The shorter inner flight feathers on the wing, which provide the lift that keeps a bird in the air.

Sibling A "brother" or "sister." In some bird species young remain with their parents when they breed again and look after their younger siblings.

Solitary Living alone for most of the time.

Species The division of animal classification below Genus; a group of animals of the same structure that can breed together.

Sub-species The division of animal classification below Species and above Race; typically the sub-species are separated into different places.

Sub-tropics The two warm regions bordering the tropics to the north and south of the equator.

Talons The sharp curved claws with which many birds of prey catch their prey.

Temperate A climate that is not too hot and not too cold. Temperate zones lie between the sub-tropics and the cold high latitude regions in both hemispheres.

Territory The area in which an animal or group of animals lives and defends against intruders.

Tropics Strictly, the region between latitudes 23° north and south of the equator. Tropical regions are typically very hot and humid.

Tundra The bleak landscape at high latitudes where the very cold climate prevents the growth of trees. A similar habitat occurs at high altitudes on mountains.

Vertebrates Animals with backbones. Fish are aquatic vertebrates and birds are terrestrial vertebrates.

INDEX

Scientific names

The first name of each double-barrel Latin name refers to the *Genus*, the second to the *species*. Single names not in *italic* refer to a family or sub-family and are cross-referenced to the Common name index.

FURTHER READING

Alexander, R. McNeill (ed) (1986), *The Encyclopedia of Animal Biology*, Facts On File, New York.

Berry, R.J. and Hallam, A (eds) (1986), *The Encyclopedia of Animal Evolution*, Facts On File, New York.

Bond, J. (1979), *Birds of the West Indies: A Guide to the Species of Birds that Inhabit the Greater Antilles, Lesser Antilles and Bahama Islands*, Collins, London.

Cramp, S. (1978-85), *Handbook of the Birds of Europe, the Middle East and North Africa: The Birds of the Western Palearctic*, vols I-IV, Oxford University Press, Oxford.

Farner, D.S., King, J.R. and Parkes, K.C.(1971-83), *Avian Biology*, vols I-VII, Academic Press, New York and London.

Farrand, J.J. (1983), *The Audubon Society Master Guide to Birding*, 3 vols, Knopf, New York.

Harrison, C.J.O. (1978), *A Field Guide to the Nests, Eggs and Nestlings of North American Birds*, Collins, London.

Moore, P.D. (ed) (1986), *The Encyclopedia of Animal Ecology*, Facts On File, New York.

National Geographic Society (1987), *Field Guide to the Birds of North America* (2nd edition), NGS, Washington.

Perrins, C.M. and Middleton, A.L.A. (eds)(1985), *The Encyclopedia of Birds*, Facts On File, New York.

Skutch, A.F. (1975), *Parent Birds and their Young*, Texas Press, Austin, Texas.

Slater, P.J.B. (ed) (1986), *The Encyclopedia of Animal Behavior*, Facts On File, New York.

Tyne, J.van and Berger, A.J. (1976), *Fundamentals of Ornithology* (2nd edition), Wiley, New York.

ACKNOWLEDGMENTS

Picture credits

Key: *t* top. *b* bottom. *c* center. *l* left. *r* right.
Abbreviations: A. Ardea. AN Agence Nature. ANT Australasian Nature Transparencies. BCL Bruce Coleman Ltd. FL Frank Lane Agency. NHPA Natural History Photographic Agency. OSF Oxford Scientific Films. PEP Planet Earth Pictures. SAL Survival Anglia Ltd.

6 A. 7 BCL/Pekka Helo. 8 BCL. 9*t*, 9*cr*, 9*br* SAL. 11*t* Len Rue Jr. 12 BCL. 13 SAL. 14 P. Morris/Ardea. 15 A. 17 NHPA. 18*tl* A. 18*cl* SAL. 19 NHPA/Nigel Dennis. 20-21 BCL. 22 Brian Hawkes. 23 SAL/D. & M. Plage. 24 Michael Fogden. 25 FL. 28 A/R J.C. Blewitt. 31 Frithfoto. 32 FL. 33*t* BCL. 33*b* NHPA. 35 PEP. 36 NHPA. 38-39 AN. 40 Heather Angel, Biofotos. 41 AN. 42 A. 43 FL/F. Merlet. 46 NHPA. 48, 49 ANT. 51 A. 53*tl*, 53*r* BCL. 54 FL. 56-57 NHPA/R.J. Erwin. 59*t* M. King & M. Read. 59*b* Nature Photographers. 60-61 NHPA 64A. 65 NHPA. 66 AN. 67 AN. 68 OSF. 69 Nature Photographers. 70 A. 71 BCL/Bob & Clara Calhoun. 76*t* NHPA. 76*b* A. 76-77 Nature Photographers. 77 BCL/H. Rivarola. 78 BCL/J. Shaw. 79A. 80 ANT. 84 A. 86 ANT. 87 NHPA. 88 A. 89 A/M.D. England.

Artwork credits

Abbreviations: DO Denys Ovenden. IW Ian Willis. ML Mick Loates. NA Norman Arlott. SD Simon Driver. SM Sean Milne. TB Trevor Boyer.

7, 9, 10, 11, 16, 18 IW. 21 Jeane Colville 23*l* IW. 23*r* Ron Hayward. 26-27 IW. 29 TB. 30-31 NA. 34 TB. 35 IW. 37 SM. 41 IW. 42, 44 SM. 49 Ron Hayward. 50-51, 52 DO. 55*bl*, 55*cr* NA. 55*br* SD. 58 NA. 62-63 SM. 66 ML. 72-73 NA. 74*l* DO. 74*r* NA. 75*t* Jeane Colville. 75*b*, 81 NA. 82 IW. 83 NA. 85 IW. 87 Jeane Colville. 89 IW.